CULINARY ARTS

PRACTICAL CAREER GUIDES

Series Editor: Kezia Endsley

Culinary Arts, by Tracy Brown Hamilton
Dental Assistants and Hygienists, by Kezia Endsley
Education Professionals, by Kezia Endsley
Health and Fitness Professionals, by Kezia Endsley
Medical Office Professionals, by Marcia Santore
Skilled Trade Professionals, by Corbin Collins

CULINARY ARTS

A Practical Career Guide

TRACY BROWN HAMILTON

ROWMAN & LITTLEFIELD
Lanham • Boulder • New York • London

Published by Rowman & Littlefield
An imprint of The Rowman & Littlefield Publishing Group, Inc.
4501 Forbes Boulevard, Suite 200, Lanham, Maryland 20706
www.rowman.com

6 Tinworth Street, London, SE11 5AL, United Kingdom

British Library Cataloguing in Publication Information Available

Library of Congress Cataloging-in-Publication Data

Names: Hamilton, Tracy Brown, 1972– author.
Title: Culinary arts : a practical career guide / Tracy Brown Hamilton.
Description: Lanham : Rowman & Littlefield, [2019] | Series: Practical career guides | Includes bibliographical references.
Identifiers: LCCN 2019000249 (print) | LCCN 2019003003 (ebook) | ISBN 9781538111741 (electronic) | ISBN 9781538111734 (pbk. : alk. paper)
Subjects: LCSH: Food service—Vocational guidance. | Cooking—Vocational guidance.
Classification: LCC TX911.3.V62 (ebook) | LCC TX911.3.V62 B76 2019 (print) | DDC 647.95023—dc23
LC record available at https://lccn.loc.gov/2019000249

Printed in the United States of America

Contents

Introduction: So You Want a Career in the Culinary Arts

*W*elcome to the field of the culinary arts! This book is the ideal start for understanding the various careers available to you within the culinary arts, which is right for you, and what path you should follow to ensure you have all the training, education, and experience needed to succeed in your future career goals.

Because the term *culinary arts* is such a broad one—there are innumerable careers that engage with the preparation and service of food, from chef to restaurateur, from caterer to food truck operator, from line chef to food photographer, and everything in between—it can be difficult and equally exciting to decide which job is the best fit for you.

A Career in the Culinary Arts

There's not nearly enough room in this book to cover all the kinds of jobs that fall within the culinary arts, but many of them require the same type of training and experience. This book will cover careers that include:

- Chefs
- Pop-up and traditional restaurant owners
- Caterers
- Media and art-related careers
- Bakers

These jobs are widely available pretty much all over the country. They pay pretty well, too, considering they don't all require that you have a college degree. And there are currently shortages of workers for these jobs. That means there are more open positions available for these jobs than there are people applying for them. That's good news for anyone looking to enter one of these professions. And the future looks bright for these jobs as well, as you'll see.

The Market Today

How does the job market look for young people seeking to enter the field of culinary arts? Although the field is a competitive one, the food and food service business is unlikely to ever lose relevance or decline. In fact, new business models—such as pop-up restaurants—are opening the field to more and more people, adding to the competition but keeping opportunities growing.

According to the Bureau of Labor Statistics (BLS), employment opportunities for chefs and head cooks is expected to grow by 10 percent between 2016 and 2026.[1] That's certainly a positive prediction—and a greater increase than most professions, which is around 7 percent. This increase is predicted to lead to 11,300 more jobs. Food preparation workers are expected to see their profession grow by 8 percent between 2016 and 2026—not as high a number, but in line with the national average for other professions.[2]

The culinary arts is a strong field with high predicted growth simply because people will always enjoy eating, be it from a diner, a fine restaurant, a food truck, an airplane, or a local café. The increase in people identifying as "foodies" is also on the rise, increasing people's interest in food innovation, constantly striving to bring more creativity and appreciation to food preparation.

A career in the culinary arts offers a broad range of creative and diverse roles.
© iStock/Getty Images Plus/Wavebreak

A greater focus on healthful eating has also paved the way for creativity, especially in using locally grown, organic ingredients and changing the way we think about food, our bodies, and our well-being. This bodes well for anyone involved in the food preparation chain, from food growers to recipe creators to chefs and those responsible for how food is presented, both on the plate and in advertising—for example, food photographers and cookbook publishers and those in other media such as television and radio programs.

According to some research, the following cities in the United States will offer the best opportunities for high-paying, secure jobs in the culinary arts:

- Denver
- San Francisco
- Washington, DC
- Bethesda, MD
- Portland, OR
- Seattle
- Los Angeles
- Philadelphia
- Chicago[3]

If you don't live near these cities or don't see yourself wanting to in the future, don't despair: Food and food service is a valuable element of any geographic location, from the smallest towns to the biggest cities, all over the world.

> "The best part [of the job] is that it feels like I'm driving this bus. The restaurant business never felt that way. Now, I decide how busy I want to be, which projects to take on, and which to pass up."—Zane Caplansky, deli man and media personality

What Does This Book Cover?

This book covers the following topics for all the aforementioned careers, as well as others:

- What kind of job best suits your personality and preference for working conditions, hours, educational requirements, work culture, and atmosphere, based on the day-to-day activities involved in each job and what a typical day at work looks like
- How to form a career plan—starting now, wherever you are in your education—and how to start taking the steps that will best lead to success
- Educational requirements and opportunities and how to fulfill them
- Writing your résumé, interviewing, networking, and applying for jobs
- Resources for further information

Once you've read the book, you will be well on your way to understanding what kind of career you want, what you can expect from it, and how to go about planning and beginning your path.

Where Do You Start?

All the jobs covered in this book require, at minimum, a high school degree or equivalent and some on-the-job training. In some cases, this will mean completing an internship, learning on the job, and completing a degree at a community college or culinary arts school. Others require a four-year degree or even a master's degree—and the subjects you should study will also vary. For example, if you want to own your own company, big or small, some business and basic accounting courses are recommended. Chemistry and other science courses can also be useful, and communication—professional and interpersonal—will also come in handy to secure you a happy and successful future.

Choosing the right career for you will also depend largely on your personality and interests outside of work—such as whether you work better with people or independently; whether you want to be the boss or work for someone you admire; what you want your life to include outside of working hours, including hobbies and other activities that are important to you; and so on.

After high school, knowing how to choose and apply to vocational training such as an apprenticeship or a college program will be the next step in your path. The information in chapter 3 will help you navigate this important stage and know what questions to ask, how to best submit yourself as a candidate, and the kinds of communication skills that are key to letting future employers or trainers understand who you are and what your potential is.

Thinking about the future and your profession is exciting and also a bit daunting. After reading this book, you will be on track toward understanding and following the steps to get yourself on the way to a happy and successful future in the culinary arts. Let's get started!

Why Choose a Career in the Culinary Arts?

*T*he fact that you are reading this book means you have decided you are interested in taking your passion for food and food preparation to the next level: considering the culinary arts as a career. Choosing a career is a difficult task, but, as will be discussed in more detail in chapter 2, there are many ways to begin gaining a solid understanding of the professional future that is most suitable and will be most satisfying to you. Of course, the first step is understanding what a particular field—in this case, the culinary arts—actually encompasses and informing yourself about how the future outlook of the profession looks. That is the emphasis of this chapter, which looks at defining the culinary arts field in general and then more specific terms, as well as examining the past and predicted future of the field.

The culinary arts, as mentioned in the introduction, is a broad umbrella that encompasses many different but related jobs. However, what can be said for the field as a whole is that it is one that offers the opportunity for experimentation, collaboration, creativity, and constant learning. If you are truly passionate about food, a career in the culinary arts will be continuously satisfying. It is also a very competitive field, often demanding long hours and entails working in high-pressure, often stressful environments. In a restaurant, you can expect lots of people bustling around under tight deadlines, relying on each other to keep pace in order to prepare and deliver a dish of quality taste and presentation to a customer's table on time. As a wedding caterer, you are under equal pressure to ensure everything goes smoothly. The job requires, therefore, a high level of organization, stress management, communication skills, and, of course, knowledge of the art and science of cooking.

So as with any career, there are pros and cons, which will be discussed later in this chapter. In balancing the good points and less attractive points of a career, you must ask yourself whether, in the end, the positive outweighs any negatives you may discover. This chapter will help you decide whether a career in the culinary arts is actually the right choice for you. And if you decide it is, the next chapter will offer suggestions about how to prepare your career path, including questions to ask yourself and resources to help you determine more specifically what kind of culinary arts career is for you.

What Are the Culinary Arts?

Although people have enjoyed eating together since the beginning of time, the formal field of the culinary arts is relatively new. Throughout history, people in China, Europe, and around the world prepared food and sold it to the public—but the official profession of chef became a reality only in more recent times. This section will look at how the field evolved from its early origins to the modern world of the culinary arts.

People have been preparing and sharing food with others throughout history, but the concept of the modern restaurant is relatively new. © iStock/Getty Images Plus/PeopleImages

THE EARLY DAYS OF COOKING AS A PROFESSION

During the sixteenth century in France, guild members—citizens belonging to an association of people with the same trade—were responsible for preparing food. Each guild was responsible for a particular food, such as, for example, a guild that had a monopoly on stews. In 1760 the first restaurant opened in Paris, operated by Monsieur Boulanger. It offered a special dish made with the feet of sheep—but his tavern was shut down after food preparation guilds that had a monopoly on such foods opposed it.

These guilds were abolished after the French Revolution, and there were no more regulations regarding who could be a butcher or a baker and so on. This opened the door for more restaurants to open in Paris, which remains one of the most important food and restaurant cities in the world today. In the United States, the term *restaurant* was not commonly used until the nineteenth century, although the notion of a business that sold food only—rather than also serving as a place for lodging—existed late in the previous century.

The origin of the term *restaurant* is often credited to Monsieur Boulanger, who offered "restorative broths" to the public in his tavern that carried the Latin motto, *Venite ad me omnes qui stomacho laboratis et ego vos restaurabo*—"Come to me all who suffer from pain of the stomach and I will restore you."[1] *Oxford English Dictionary's Historical Thesaurus* includes six terms that refer to an establishment serving food: *eating house*, *victualling-house*, *cook's shop*, *treating-house*, *suttling-house*, and *chop shop*.

It was the Industrial Revolution, a period of rapid advancement in manufacturing and transportation that occurred between 1760 and 1840, that had a great impact on how food was prepared, produced, and distributed. According to the authors of *On Cooking: A Textbook of Culinary Fundamentals*, "The dramatic growth and diversification of the food service industry is due in part to the Industrial Revolution and the social and economic changes it wrought, including the introduction of new technologies, foods, concerns, and consumers."[2]

Some other key milestones in the development of the culinary arts as a profession include:

- *1783–1833:* Grande cuisine—also called haute cuisine—a style of cooking that emphasizes high-quality taste and presentation, was developed by Antonin Carême, a chef who specialized in this posh and complicated style. He is also credited with developing other advancements, such as a system for classifying sauces and cooking equipment and tools.
- *1846–1935:* Auguste Escoffier created the brigade system, which defines the hierarchy of large kitchens in hotels and restaurants that hire many staff. See sidebar "Understanding the Kitchen Brigade" for more details.
- *1897–1955:* Nouvelle cuisine—which focuses on innovation of ingredient combinations, a shorter cooking time, and more natural flavors—was created by Fernand Point, a French chef, along with several of his cooking students.
- *1903:* French chef Auguste Escoffier produced *Le Guide Culinaire Classic*, a manual that explained and streamlined French cooking of his day.

UNDERSTANDING THE KITCHEN BRIGADE

In 1889 the Savoy Hotel opened its doors in London, England. It was the first luxury eating establishment of its type in England and French chef Auguste Escoffier was brought onboard as its restaurant's head *chef de cuisine*, or executive chef. Escoffier, who had served in the French military, wanted to devise a system of hierarchy in the kitchen to ensure an efficient working environment in which every employee knew exactly what he or she was responsible for and where each person in the kitchen staff ranked as far as authority. Hence the kitchen brigade was born—an exhaustive outline that included more than twenty positions. In the modern restaurant, many of these original positions have been eliminated or combined, streamlining the process even further. Although the term kitchen brigade is still widely used, it now refers most often to the following general positions—ranked here from highest to lowest in the chain:

- *Chef de cuisine:* This is the highest position in the modern kitchen. The chef de cuisine is in charge of everything from menu preparation to ordering ingredients.

- *Sous chef de cuisine:* In the French language, *sous* means *under*—making the sous chef a sort of deputy to the chef de cuisine. The sous chef is second in command in the kitchen, taking over the responsibilities of the head chef in his or her absence.
- *Chef de partie:* A chef de partie—there are several in a professional kitchen—is a chef who is responsible for a particular station. There will be several parties—such as a fish chef, vegetable chef, sauté chef, or pastry chef. Parties often have a cuisinier, commis, or apprentices working with them.
- *Cuisinier:* The cuisiniers do the actual cooking at a specific station.
- *Commis:* The commis is a junior cook assigned to a particular station who most often is responsible for ensuring the proper cooking equipment is present at his or her station.
- *Apprentice:* An apprentice is a person who is working to gain experience and who generally does anything from prep work to washing dishes.[3]

With so many people working in a busy kitchen, a hierarchy of command keeps things running smoothly. © *iStock/Getty Images Plus/JazzIRT*

THE MODERN-DAY CULINARY ARTS

Today, the culinary arts is a thriving career field, full of variety and possibility. Although most people may associate the culinary arts with the job of chef, there are many other functions—anything from cheesemaker to baker—that are also included in the culinary arts. Because every step in the chain of food preparation—from farming to purchasing ingredients to cooking dishes to serving them—is considered part of the culinary arts, the possibilities for career choices are innumerable.

Although this book will cover as many of these careers as possible, it will focus mostly on the following:

- *Chef:* A chef is a person who prepares food in a kitchen. It is a broad term—anyone from an executive chef, who directs the kitchen, to a line cook is considered a chef. Chapter 3 will look at the differences among the various types of chef more closely.
- *Pop-up and traditional restaurant owners:* This includes anyone running a food-service business, be it a Michelin-starred restaurant or an ice cream stand.
- *Caterers:* Caterers can work anywhere, from their own homes to large corporations, preparing food for parties, functions, and other events and delivering and serving food on-site.
- *Media and art-related careers:* Not all culinary art professionals actually prepare food in the traditional sense. This book will also discuss media-related careers such as cookbook authors (who are, of course, expert cooks) and food photographers and food stylists, who work with edible and nonedible materials to prepare "food" to be photographed or to appear in television advertising.
- *Bakers:* The culinary arts professionals who satisfy a sweet tooth or provide freshly baked bread early in the morning cannot be forgotten. Bakers and pastry chefs are a key part of the culinary arts, and the job possibilities are numerous.

Michelin stars are awarded to restaurants of high quality. One to three Michelin stars can be awarded—one star means "a very good restaurant in its category"; two stars mean "excellent cooking, worth a detour"; and three stars mean "exceptional cuisine, worth a special journey." Each year, the *Michelin Guide* is published ranking top restaurants around the world.[4]

The Pros and Cons of the Culinary Arts Field

As with any career, one in the culinary arts has upsides and downsides. But also true is that one person's pro is another person's con. If you love waking up in the early morning hours, then that is a definite positive to working in a bakery, where you will get to work creating fresh baked goods before the sun comes up. It can also mean working weekends. For some people, this is a positive, but those who like to sleep a little longer and take the weekends off should consider that reality before launching a baking career.

Although it's one thing to read about the pros and cons of a particular career, the best way to really get a feel for what a typical day is like on the job and what the challenges and rewards are is to talk to someone who is already working in the profession or who has in the past.

Although each profession within the culinary arts is different, there are some generalizations that can be made when it comes to what is most challenging and most gratifying about the field.

Here are some general pros:

- The work tends to be creative and challenging.
- In this competitive field, you will have colleagues who share your passion and from whom you can learn.
- The career outlook is very good! See the next section for more about this.
- It is a constantly evolving field with new trends and innovations and endless opportunity for learning.
- Every day is different, and there's no sitting in a cubicle in front of a computer for hours on end.
- There's a great variety in work environments, from large corporations to entrepreneurial opportunities.
- It's a field you can enter without necessarily needing a college degree.
- Depending on where you work, salaries can be quite lucrative. For example, a chef in a large restaurant, hotel, or spa can expect to make a good living.

And here are some general cons:

- The working hours—particularly for chefs, caterers, bakers, and restaurant owners—can be very irregular. You can expect to work weekends and evenings, or, in the case of bakers, very early in the mornings.
- The work can be physically exhausting—with long hours on your feet—and also a little dangerous, because working in a hectic kitchen with ovens and stoves, sharp objects, and slippery floors can lead to a lot of accidents.
- It is a high-pressure field that requires an ability to be flexible and manage stress well, as well as to multitask.
- It is an extremely competitive field, and advancing to the next level can take a lot of time, hard work, and patience.
- Although some careers in the culinary arts offer lucrative salaries, as mentioned above, many do not—particularly when you are just starting out.

> "I really enjoy the collaboration on most jobs. Getting to work with other creatives, bouncing ideas off each other and being inspired by their vision. . . . I also love to shop. I have a thing for collecting ceramics that I sometimes wonder borders on obsession. Luckily this job provides good cover for that."—Glenn Jenkins, food photographer

How Healthy Is the Job Market for the Culinary Arts?

For the most part, the career outlook for the culinary arts is very healthy. For one thing, people will always want to gather to eat, but in recent years people are increasingly interested in learning about and preparing healthier and more innovative foods—be it at home, in a fancy restaurant, or at a simple diner. This means there is plenty of room for more creative, inventive professionals in the field of the culinary arts.

At the same time, it's a competitive field, and hard work and long hours are often required. Still, when compared with other careers in the United States, the Bureau of Labor Statistics predicts positive growth—in some cases above the average for all careers—for the job market in the culinary arts.[5] Below are statistics published by the BLS about specific careers in the field. Note that the BLS did not release statistics for all careers that fall under the culinary arts umbrella.

CHEFS AND HEAD COOKS

Chefs and head cooks are responsible for supervising the preparation of food and managing and directing the rest of the kitchen staff. They work anywhere food is served, from restaurants to cruise ships to private homes.

- *Hourly pay:* $22.09
- *Annual wage:* $45,950
- *Projected growth 2016–2026:* 10 percent (faster than average)

According to Payscale.com, the average annual wage for an executive chef is $58.807, but this can be much higher in major cities like Washington, DC, or New York City.[6]

LINE COOK

Line cooks work in restaurants, schools, diners, hospitals, and anywhere else where food is served. They are tasked with preparing, seasoning, and cooking a range of foods, from soup to salad to main courses to desserts.

- *Hourly pay:* $11.52
- *Annual wage:* $23,970
- *Projected growth 2016–2026:* 6 percent (as fast as average)

FOOD SERVICE MANAGERS

Food service managers oversee the daily operation of restaurants and other places where food is prepared or served, such as cafeterias, hotels, or schools. They manage the rest of the kitchen staff to ensure customer satisfaction and manage the business as a whole to ensure it is profitable.

- *Hourly pay:* $25.02
- *Annual wage:* $52,030
- *Projected growth 2016–2026:* 9 percent (as fast as average)

FOOD AND BEVERAGE SERVING AND RELATED WORKERS

Food and beverage serving and related workers are responsible for a variety of tasks, from customer service, food preparation, and cleaning duties. They work in restaurants, cafeterias, and other eating and drinking establishments.

- *Hourly pay:* $9.81
- *Annual wage:* $20,410
- *Projected growth 2016–2026:* 14 percent (faster than average)

BAKERS

Bakers have the delicious task of mixing ingredients to make baked goods, from breads to cakes to pastries. Some bakers specialize in things like wedding cakes, and they can work anywhere from supermarkets to specialized bakery shops.

A growing number of bakers are dabbling in the freelance world.[7] As a freelance baker, you don't have to work in a bakery or supermarket or any other place of business, and you can set your own hours. By promoting your own home-based business by word of mouth and the Internet (think video tutorials of your recipes or social media such as Pinterest), you can gain connections—and customers—and sell your baked goods from your home.

- *Hourly pay:* $12.35
- *Annual wage:* $25,690
- *Projected growth 2016–2026:* 6 percent (slower than average)

FOOD PHOTOGRAPHERS

Food photographers are artists who capture images of foods to be used in magazines, newspapers, websites, menus, and anywhere else food or the establishment serving or selling it wants to advertise. A food photographer has a keen eye for making food look delicious and attractive as possible.

- *Hourly pay:* $15.62
- *Annual wage:* $32,490
- *Projected growth 2016–2026:* 8 percent (as fast as average)

A food photographer often works alongside a food stylist. It is the job of the food stylist to make the food beautiful and presentable before it is photographed or filmed, usually for an advertisement. Sometimes real food is not even used—instead other materials or ingredients, edible or not, are styled to look like the food they represent.

CAREER AND TECHNICAL EDUCATION TEACHERS IN THE CULINARY ARTS

Career and technical education teachers instruct in what are called vocational subjects, which means any training in skills for a specific occupation, including in the culinary arts. A career as a culinary arts instructor could see you training students in a culinary arts school or community college.

- *Hourly pay:* Not listed
- *Annual wage:* $55,240
- *Projected growth 2016–2026:* 4 percent (slower than average)

Am I Right for a Culinary Arts Career?

Whether you are a good match for a career in the culinary arts is a tough question to answer, because the answer can only come from you. But don't despair: There are plenty of resources, both online and elsewhere, that can help you find the answer by guiding you through the questions and considerations that will bring you to your conclusion. These are covered in more detail in chapter 2. But for now, let's look at the general demands and responsibilities of a culinary arts career—as mentioned previously in the section on pros and cons—and look at some questions that may help you discover whether such a profession is a good match for your personality, interests, and the general lifestyle you want in the future.

Of course, no job is going to perfectly match your personality or fit your every desire, especially when you are just starting out. There are, however, some aspects to a job that may be so unappealing or simply mismatched that you may decide to opt for something else; you may also be so drawn to one feature of a job that any downsides are not that important to you.

Obviously, having a talent and a passion for cooking or baking or working with food preparation in any capacity is key to success in this field, but there are other factors to keep in mind. One way to see if you may be cut out for a career in the skilled trades is to ask yourself the following questions:

- *Would I prefer to be active and moving around during work, or would I rather mostly stay put behind a desk?* Working in a kitchen means standing for long hours at a time. Equally, cooking work—be it as a chef, caterer, baker, and so on—can entail heavy lifting. It's important to have the mental and physical stamina to be able to work long hours many days in a row doing creative but physical labor, sometimes in dangerous conditions—accidents in crowded kitchens can occur frequently.
- *When something goes wrong, can I think quickly on my feet to find a solution? Do I have the leadership skills to direct others to problem-solve?* Particularly as a head or executive chef, restaurant owner, or private business owner, when things go wrong you will be called on to solve the problem quickly, effectively, and with as little transparency as possible. Customers will not want to know why their food is late or prepared badly; if something goes wrong, you have to be able to resolve it without it becoming obvious to your customer or client.
- *Am I able to follow directions even if I don't agree? Am I able to understand instructions quickly?* A kitchen is a tightly run ship. Particularly in a kitchen for a large establishment like a hotel, there is a set hierarchy of who is in charge and who must follow the commands of another person. Kitchens are also hurried environments where there is little time for discussion or debate. If you are the type of person who prefers to be self-directed and in charge, then perhaps you are better suited to run your own business than to work in a busy kitchen.
- *Can I see myself owning my own business one day?* Related to the previous question, wanting to run your own business entails more than just wanting to be in charge. You will have a great responsibility for

everything from designing your business model to hiring staff to advertising and purchasing and managing stock. A lot rests on your shoulders as a business owner.

- *Can I consistently deal with people in a professional, friendly way?* This will be relevant no matter what area of the culinary arts appeals to you. Customer service is an integral part of food service and preparation, be it at a supermarket deli or a five-star restaurant. Being able to work with people, especially when there's conflict to resolve, in a professional and effective manner, is crucial. Equally, the way you communicate with your colleagues, superiors, and anyone working for you will be absolutely crucial in how successful you will be. Kitchens are hectic work environments, so communicating what is needed quickly and clearly is essential, and there will be no time for arguments or confusion.

TAKING A CHANCE ON A HOT DOG VENTURE

Christopher Collins.
*Courtesy of
Christopher Collins*

Christopher Collins took a surprisingly indirect path in launching a career in the culinary arts as the owner of a hog dog business, Lucky Louie's Sausage and Hot Dogs, in his home city of Indianapolis, Indiana. Here he shares his insights on launching a business in a brand-new field—his previous experience was in publishing and the nonprofit sector—what he learned about the food and business world, and what he plans to do next.

What led you to a career in the hot dog vendor business?

I had been working in the nonprofit field for about fifteen years, and if there is such a thing as a nonprofit rat race, I was in it. Although sometimes fulfilling—I worked in youth development and community development at the macro level—I couldn't shake the notion that all I really did was sit around in meetings. And most of those meetings went nowhere. No action, no progress, no fun. So, one day, I was bored and clicked around the web until I could legitimately go to lunch. I found one of those Top 10 Jobs That Make Surprisingly Good Money lists, and there it was: Hot Dog Vendor. It stopped me in my tracks.

I live in a city of just under 1 million people, and we have a pretty vibrant food truck scene. However, the more I researched, the more I realized that what was missing in the mobile food landscape was a high-quality hot dog and sausage option. My initial idea was to simply create a high-end hot dog cart. The carts that trolled around downtown were pretty nasty—supermarket hot dogs, stale condiments, and carts held together with duct tape. I wanted to turn all that around. But the deeper I got into the food truck scene, it became clear that I needed to think bigger and do the full-on food truck. My wife agreed. "So, are you really going to stand around in February in sub-zero degrees at a hot dog cart?" Good question.

Fast forward six months, and I had purchased a brand-new vending trailer, a pickup truck, and a 3,000-watt generator. Oh, and I put in my two weeks' notice. I was all in. The night before my first shift out (a lunch shift across the street from a large construction site), I got sick. It was nerves. What was I doing? Why was I doing this? Friends and family kept assuring me that this was going to be a cool thing to do, but the number of hoops through which you have to jump to actually make it happen was enormous. If you do it right, launching a food truck is a lot like opening a tiny restaurant. Permits, insurance, fees, health codes, commissary agreements, storage . . . it really does go on and on.

What is it like launching a business as an entrepreneur?

I think I made $42 that first lunch shift. I had also hired an employee, so actually I think I made closer to $12. Slowly but surely, I started to learn the business. The most unique thing about running a hot dog food truck is that, unlike the vast majority of other kinds of foods, hot dogs and sausages aren't rocket science. It's the dog, the bun, and the toppings. I worked a long time to streamline my menu so I could do it all myself. The only other things I offered were (above average) chips and soft drinks. I started using my employee less and less, and finally realized that the only time I needed help was during large events. I could do most festivals alone—I could serve 150 people by myself, no problem.

But I also began to dive deeper into my QuickBooks when I just couldn't figure out where my money was going. The more I made, the more everything cost. I kept having increasingly better years, but my expenses crept up right along with everything else. One of the ways that you get "ahead" in the food truck world is to work, work, and work some more. And honestly, that's not the reason I got into it. I had thought that I could carve out a profitable niche by offering office workers a great lunch alternative. But to really make money—or at least, a small profit—you have to work every Thursday, Friday, and Saturday night. And that's not something I was willing to do with a lovely wife and a toddler at home. At the same time, I noticed other food truck owners (we are a tight brother- and sisterhood) continually sniffing around my truck, most with the same question: "How do you do it all yourself?" The majority of truck owners have to hire help, and that eats into any profit (unless they're family) very quickly.

After the third year, I started to float the idea of selling. Another food truck owner, who ran a pretty standard comfort food concept, finally got serious with me about buying my setup. It took about three months of negotiation, but in the end, we settled on an amount—basically a lease option, where he paid me a monthly fee with the goal of buying me out in the end. Fortunately, the deal went smoothly, and now, every once in a while, I'll grab a hot dog from my old food truck. It's weird, but it's also kind of cool.

What was a typical day in your job?

There were really only a few types of days: days where you just do a lunch shift, days where you do a lunch and dinner shift, or days where you do a festival or event. Festivals aren't typical, so on a typical lunch and dinner day, you start by hooking up your vending trailer to your truck. Of course, you typically don't park your food truck or trailer at your house, so you go to your storage facility. Then you head to your commissary, the commercial kitchens out of which food trucks are required to operate. This is where you make, store, and package all of your products. From there, I would head out to my lunch spot. By my second year, I generally had every day of the month scheduled prior to that month starting. It was up to me how much I wanted to work. Once at your spot, you set up and you serve. After lunch, you package up the food that you could reuse, and you either head back to the commissary or you stop by the food supply store to replenish depleted product. By then, it's around 2:00 p.m., and you head home or somewhere to respond to e-mails and calls, and continue to work on your schedule, menu, and social media presence.

What was the best part of your job?

The best part, by far, was seeing how happy people were with the food I served. For whatever reasons, people have strong opinions about hot dogs, in particular, and getting a compliment from a true north side Chicago-ite about my Chicago Dog literally made my week. It reminded me that I was doing it right. I would have put my dogs up against any in the city, and it was the enthusiasm from customers that made the job, at times, joyous.

What was the worst part of your job?

You get booked for a gig where the promoter promises at least two hundred people. You prep, you buy extra product, and you might even invite someone to help out. And twenty-five people show up. That is absolutely the worst scenario in the food truck world.

What was the most surprising thing about your job?

I was always surprised by how much people who invite food trucks to their offices or organize food truck events (the people who hire you) overthink it. Often, you'd see a live band over there, kids' games over there, the beer tent over there, and the food trucks *way* over there. It's really not rocket science. You put the food trucks near the beer and other fun. It's really that simple.

What's next? Where do you see yourself going from here?

Owning a food truck really meant that I got bit by the entrepreneurial bug. I knew that it was possible to run a small business while finding a better profit margin. I understood so much better the things that make a small business click. While I was selling the truck, I had connected with a company that was expanding its BBQ grill cleaning business. It seemed like a great opportunity, and after about six months of due diligence, I bought the system.

Did your education prepare you for the job?

I have a bachelor's degree in journalism and a master's degree in social work. It seems a little strange, but I would say that both have contributed to why I consider the two businesses I've started a success. I quickly realized that culinary people make food their top priority. And rightly so, I suppose. But customers and clients really value basic communication skills. I couldn't believe how grateful people were when I would do something as simple as return a phone call. I used my journalism and writing experience to produce all of my marketing materials and create a compelling brand that ultimately led to someone actually wanting to buy my business. My social work background informed me of the value of linking your business to a greater good. Giving 10 percent of your profits to the neighborhood fund in which you're working is always a good thing.

Is the job what you expected?

As I said a little bit previously, I hadn't expected how much you really have to work to make a living running a food truck. Nights, weekends—you have to work when people go out to eat.

Summary

This chapter covered a lot of ground as far as looking more closely at the various types of professions and jobs that exist within the overarching field of the culinary arts. Because the culinary arts involve anything to do with food production, preparation, and delivery, there are an endless number of jobs that are required along the way, from food growers to restaurant servers. Because of this, covering every culinary arts career is beyond the scope of this chapter, but most of the information is relevant to the field as a whole. This chapter instead looked at some specific culinary arts jobs, such as chef and baker, including statistics on career prospects and growth over time.

And the field of the culinary arts is constantly evolving: This chapter looked far back in history at how food preparation has been handled over time, from guilds to the explosion of the restaurant industry around the world. And with a growing awareness of ways to grow, cook, and eat food—think about the rise in organic ingredients or fusion cooking—people are becoming more and more interested in food and food innovation all the time.

Here are some ideas to take away with you as you move on to the next chapter:

- The field of the culinary arts is a broad one that continues to evolve, as it has ever since it first became a profession hundreds of years ago. That makes it an exciting and open field, with loads of room for creativity and experimentation.
- No day in a culinary arts career is the same. You can expect pleasant and less pleasant surprises, irregular schedules, long hours, and lots of activity. It can be tiring, but never dull.
- The BLS predicts healthy growth for many roles within the culinary arts, including that of chef and head chef. In some cases, because people will always enjoy having a meal outside of the home and more restaurants are cropping up all the time, job growth is predicted to be higher than the average for other professions in the United States.
- Given all you now know about culinary arts professions, you may still be questioning whether such a career is right for you. This chapter provided some questions that can help you visualize yourself in real-world situations you can expect to face on the job, such as whether you see

yourself taking or giving orders, whether you can stand for hours at a time, and how strong your communication skills are. These are all very important factors of how successful you will be, no matter how well you can cook or bake.

Assuming you are now more enthusiastic than ever about pursuing a career in the culinary arts, the next chapter will look more closely at how you can refine your choice to a more specific job. It offers tips and advice about how to find the role and work environment that will be most satisfying to you and what steps you can start taking—immediately!—toward reaching your future career goals.

Chefs preparing dinner. © *iStock/Getty Images Plus/pidjoe*

2

Forming a Career Plan

Choosing a career is one of the most important decisions you will make in your life. With so many career choices available, it is easy to feel overwhelmed. Particularly if you have many passions and interests, it can be hard to narrow your options down. That you are reading this book means you have decided to investigate a career in the culinary arts, which means you have already discovered a passion for food and cooking. But even within the culinary arts, there are many choices, including what role you want to pursue, what work environment you desire, and what type of work schedule best fits your lifestyle.

The culinary arts in general terms refers to the preparation of food, and many people associate it mostly with being a chef or owning a restaurant. It is, however, far broader than that. Within the culinary arts are career choices ranging from nutritionist to personal chef to caterer. People with degrees in the culinary arts can go on to work as food stylists for advertising and publishing companies. They can work as food scientists, conducting research to improve public safety when it relates to food.

Before you can plan the path to a successful career in the culinary arts, it's helpful to develop an understanding of what role you want to have and in what environment you wish to work. Do you see yourself working as a line cook in a local diner, for example, or preparing pastries in a bustling bakery? Are you interested in owning your own catering business or working as a culinary instructor? Developing a deeper understanding of what kind of career you want in the food business will help you know what path to follow to achieve your goal most effectively.

Depending on your ultimate career goal, the steps to getting there differ. Some jobs require certification from a culinary arts school, while others require an associate's or bachelor's degree. Most require work experience via an internship training program or an apprenticeship. In some cases—for example, if you aspire to run your own food-related business or work as a food scientist—courses outside of the area of cooking—business and science classes, for example—may also be required. Your own personal qualities are also a large factor in preparing yourself for your ideal career. Strong networking and inter-personal skills, for example, will be invaluable in entering and succeeding in this competitive field.

Deciding on a career means asking yourself big questions, but there are sev-eral tools and assessments that can help you determine your personal strengths and aptitudes and with which career fields and environments they best align. These tools guide you to think about important factors in choosing a career path, such as how you respond to pressure and how effectively—and how much you enjoy—working and communicating with people.

This chapter explores the educational requirements for various careers within the culinary arts, as well as options for where to go for help when plan-ning your path to the career you want. It offers advice on how to begin pre-paring for your career path at any age or stage in your education, including in high school. It covers certifications and options for how to gain work experi-ence, which will not only improve your skills and culinary know-how but will give you an idea of what a typical day in the life of a culinary arts professional looks like and what kind of job is the best fit for you.

Planning the Plan

So where to begin? Before taking the leap and applying to a culinary arts school, there are other considerations and steps you can take to map out your plan for pursing your career. Preparing your career plan begins with developing a clear understanding of what your actual career goal is.

Planning your career path means asking yourself questions that will help shape a clearer picture of what your long-term career goals are and what steps you should take in order to achieve them. When considering these questions, it's important to prioritize your answers—when listing your skills, for example, put them in order of strongest to weakest. When considering questions related to how you want to balance your career with your nonwork life, such as family and hobbies, really think about what your top priorities are and in what order.

The following questions and considerations are helpful to think about deeply when planning your career path.

- Think about your interests outside of the work context. How do you like to spend your free time? What inspires you? What kind of people do you like to surround yourself with? How do you best learn? What do you really love doing?
- Brainstorm a list of the various career choices within the culinary arts you are interested in pursuing. Organize the list in order of which careers you find most appealing, and then list what it is about each that attracts you. This can be anything from work environment to geographical location to the degree to which you would work with other people in a particular role.
- Research information on each job on your career choices list. You can find job descriptions, salary indications, career outlook, salary, and educational requirements online, for example.
- Consider your personality traits. How do you respond to stress and pressure? Do you consider yourself a strong communicator? Do you work well in teams or do you prefer to work independently? Do you consider yourself creative? How do you respond to criticism? All of these are important to keep in mind to ensure you choose a career path that makes you happy and in which you can thrive.
- Although a career choice is obviously a huge factor in your future, it's important to consider what other factors feature into your vision of your ideal life. Think about how your career will fit in with the rest of your life, including whether you want to live in a big city or small town, how much flexibility you want in your schedule, how much autonomy you want in your work, and what your ultimate career goal is.
- The culinary arts can be a very competitive field, particularly when you are starting out in your career. Because it requires so much commitment, it's important to think about how willing you are to put in long hours and perform what can be physically demanding work. If you want to own your own food-related business, think about how much risk you are comfortable taking.
- While there are many lucrative careers in the culinary arts field, many job opportunities that offer experience to newcomers and recent culinary art school graduates come with relatively low salaries. What are your pay expectations, now and in the future?

Making a decision about what kind of career to pursue can be much simpler if you ask yourself some key questions. © iStock/Getty Images Plus/FlamingoImages

Posing these questions to yourself and thinking about them deeply and answering them honestly will help make your career goals clearer and guide you in knowing which steps you will need to take to get there.

CULINARY CAREERS THAT DON'T REQUIRE COOKING

A culinary arts career demands that you have a passion for food and food preparation. Most people entering the field—be it as a pastry chef or line cook—also have a talent and deep interest in cooking. Not all jobs within the culinary arts arena, however, require that you have excellent cooking skills—or even any at all.

There are several career options within the food preparation and service industry that have little to do with cooking itself. Here are a few examples:

- *Food stylists and photographers* are culinary professionals whose job it is to ensure food looks irresistibly good before being filmed or photographed, such as for advertisements or cookbooks. Often what is being photographed is not what it is supposed to be. Tricks such as using motor oil as chocolate sauce or using a blowtorch to brown a piece of meat are common in food styling and photography.

- *Restaurant promoters* play an important role in the food industry. The core task of a restaurant promoter is to perform public relations for a restaurant, hotel, or spa, for example. Promoters help food-related business stay competitive and successful by organizing events, writing press releases, and attracting new business.
- *Beverage managers* work in restaurants, hotels, spas, and so on, and are responsible for the organization of drinks. This includes how beverages are stored and presented as well as what beverages are available and at what price. The beverage manager is also in charge of ordering and tracking beverage inventory as well as training bar staff.

Where to Go for Help

The process of deciding on and planning a career path is daunting. In many ways, the range of career choices available today is a wonderful thing. It allows us to refine our career goals and customize them to our own lives and personalities. In other ways, though, too much choice can be extremely daunting, and require a lot of soul-searching to navigate clearly.

Answering questions about your habits, characteristics, interests, and personality can be very challenging. Identifying and prioritizing all of your ambitions, interests, and passions can be overwhelming and complicated. It's not always easy to see ourselves objectively or see a way to achieve what matters most to us. But there are several resources and approaches to help guide you in drawing conclusions about these important questions.

- Take a career assessment test to help you answer questions about what career best suits you. There are several available online, many specifically for careers in the culinary arts.
- Consult with a career or personal coach to help you refine your understanding of your goals and how to pursue them.

- Talk with professionals working in the job you are considering and ask them what they enjoy about their work, what they find the most challenging, and what path they followed to get there.
- Educate yourself as much as possible about food and food prep. Learn, for example, the various types of potatoes and for what dishes they are best suited. Become fluent in spices and sauces. The more knowledge you have about foods, flavors, and presentation, the better prepared you will be for a career in the food industry.
- If possible, arrange to shadow someone working in the field you are considering. This will enable you to experience in person what the atmosphere is like, what a typical workday entails, how coworkers interact with each other and with management, and how well you can see yourself thriving in that role and work culture.
- Gain work experience by working in a restaurant in any capacity, including as a dishwasher or as a server, to get a feeling for the culture, energy, and demands of working in the restaurant business.
- Follow online tutorials or take lessons in basic cooking skills, such as prepping produce, fish, and meats. Look for courses available at local community colleges or cooking schools, or ask someone you know who is skilled in the kitchen to help you learn basic techniques such as which knives to use for different tasks and how to use them correctly, or how to equip a basic kitchen.

ONLINE RESOURCES TO HELP YOU PLAN YOUR PATH

The internet is an excellent source of advice and assessment tools that can help you find and figure out how to pursue your career path. Some of these tools focus on personality and aptitude, while others can help you identify and improve your skills to prepare for your career.

In addition to the sites listed, you can also use the internet to find a career or life coach near you—many offer their services online as well. Job sites such as LinkedIn are a good place to search for people working in a profession you'd like to learn more about, or to explore the types of jobs available in the culinary arts.

- At educations.com, you will find a career test designed to help you find the job of your dreams. Visit www.educations.com/career-test to take the test.
- The website e-rcps.com provides not only a range of easy-to-make recipes but also a quiz you can take to assess whether a career in the culinary arts is for you. You can take the quiz here: www.e-rcps.com/learn.
- The Princeton Review has created a career quiz that focuses on personal interests: www.princetonreview.com/quiz/career-quiz.
- The Bureau of Labor Statistics (BLS) provides information, including quizzes and videos, to help students up to grade 12 explore various career paths. The site also provides general information on career prospects and salaries, for example, for various jobs in the culinary arts and other fields. Visit http://bls.gov to find these resources.

Young adults with disabilities can face additional challenges when planning a career path. DO-IT (Disabilities, Opportunities, Internetworking, and Technology) is an organization dedicated to promoting career and education inclusion for everyone. Its website contains a wealth of information and tools to help all young people plan a career path, including self-assessment tests and career exploration questionnaires.[1]

Making High School Count

Once you have discovered your passion and have a fairly strong idea what type of career you want to pursue, you will naturally want to start putting your career path plan into motion as quickly as you can. If you are a high school student, you may feel there isn't much you can do toward achieving your career goals—other than, of course, earning good grades and graduating. But there are actually many ways you can make your high school years count toward your career in culinary arts before you have earned your high school diploma. This section will cover how you can use this period of your education and life to better prepare you for your career goal and to ensure you keep your passion alive while improving your skill set.

Even while still in high school, there are many ways you can begin working toward your career goal. © *iStock/Getty Images Plus/DMEPhotography*

COURSES TO TAKE IN HIGH SCHOOL

Depending on your high school and what courses you have access to, there are many subjects that will help you prepare for a career in the culinary arts. If you go to a school that offers cooking courses, that's obviously a good place to start. However, there are other courses and subjects that are just as relevant to a culinary career. Some of them may seem unrelated initially, but they will all help you prepare yourself and develop key skills.

- *Language arts:* If you work as a chef, it's very important to have strong language skills to be able to interpret and write recipes—perhaps even cookbooks, blogs, and articles. Restaurant and other big and small business owners—be it in catering or working as a personal chef—have better success if they can communicate well what services they provide and describe both services and products in a way that draws customers.

- *Math:* Knowing how to measure ingredients and make calculations for recipes is important for any type of chef or cook. Converting recipes from grams to ounces, for example, requires math savvy, as does altering recipes when ingredients need to be doubled to accommodate a larger serving size. And if you aim to own your own business, math is definitely essential for working with budgets and managing profits and losses, among other tasks.

- *Interpersonal communication/public speaking:* Working in the culinary arts in any capacity requires strong, clear communication. In a hectic kitchen with many staff working under tight pressure often in a small space, sharing information effectively and efficiently—and most of all with clarity—is crucial.

- *Science:* Chefs use science in many ways in their work. Chemistry helps a chef understand how different ingredients react with one another. When you heat sugar and it caramelizes, that is an example of a chemical reaction. If you want to work as a food scientist, knowledge of biology is required.

- *Art:* Food photographers and food stylists certainly rely on their artistic flair to produce the best images of the most beautiful and appealing foods. Cake decorators and pastry chefs equally possess a strong eye for art and design, as well as the skills to execute them. Food presentation—how food is served on a plate—is also a very important part of the cooking and eating experience, and demands artistic creativity.

- *Nutrition and wellness:* These classes focus on basic cooking skills and nutrition. With an ever-growing focus on healthful eating and wellness and with the growing popularity of the farm-to-table movement, which encourages serving locally grown foods in restaurants and cafeterias, increased awareness of the nutritional value and the origin of ingredients is fundamental.

- *Business and economics:* As with any type of business, if you have the ambition to run your own—be it a chain of restaurants or a food truck—knowledge gained in business and economics classes will prepare you to make smarter business and financial decisions.

Depending on where you live, you may find culinary arts schools with programs specifically designed for high school students. The Culinary Institute of America, for example, offers a two-day program for high school juniors who wish to apply to culinary arts school after earning their high school diploma. Participants have the opportunity to explore the state-of-the art kitchens and learn about career possibilities and of course take cooking courses. Cooking classes and camps exist in many states as well. Search online for cooking and culinary arts–related programs for young adults near you.

GAINING WORK EXPERIENCE

The best way to learn anything is to do it. When it comes to preparing for a career in the culinary arts, there are several options for gaining real-world experience and get a feel for whether you are choosing the right career for you.

In whatever capacity—as a dishwasher, server, and so on—spending time in a restaurant environment will be very educational. It will give you a chance to experience the atmosphere, how the business is operated, what the hours are, and how various employees interact with one another during a typical work day. Celebrity chef, healthy food activist, and cookbook author Jamie Oliver has credited his passion and skills for cooking with working in his parent's pub when he was a child.

Volunteering for organizations such as Meals on Wheels, which prepare and deliver food to people who are unable to do so for themselves, is another way to gain experience in a kitchen. Food purchasing and preparation—especially for a large group of people—is a valuable skill to hone. Meal centers provide another good way to experience working in a team to produce and serve food to large groups of people.

Arrange to shadow with a culinary arts professional in whichever capacity you find most interesting to you. This means accompanying someone to work, observing the tasks they perform, the work culture, the environment, the hours, and the intensity of the work. Talk with people you know who work in the food business about their job and what advice they can offer you to prepare yourself for that career track.

DEVELOPING A GREEN THUMB

Food preparation begins with growing the right ingredients. It may seem far fetched, but gardening skills are becoming increasingly valuable in the culinary arts world. Locally grown, organic fruits, herbs, and vegetables are in high demand as the farm-to-table movement continues to gain momentum.

Knowing more about how foods are grown and in which season and geographical location certain foods are produced is valuable to anyone who cooks. It can not only ensure your creations taste the best and are healthy and organic, but it can also inspire creative, seasonal recipes unique to where you live.

To gain experience gardening, you can start simply by growing your own herbs. You can also find out if your community has a communal gardening initiative in which volunteers grow and share food. Even if you don't do your own gardening, try visiting your local farmer's market to get a sense of what food is grown in your area and when, and to talk with the people who grow it.

Educational Requirements

There are several educational options for becoming a chef. Many people who eventually become chefs begin in an entry-level role such as a line chef, chopping and preparing ingredients. Additional education is not officially required, but in a competitive field such as this, it is a good idea to consider pursuing further qualifications.

In addition to the educational requirements listed here, based on information provided by the BLS, on-site training to gain real-world experience is invaluable to culinary arts careers directly related to cooking and food preparation or working in any environment where food is served, such as hotels, restaurants, schools, and even airplanes.

- *Chefs and head cooks, including personal chefs:* For the most part, chefs and head cooks improve their skills with work experience. Many others further their training at community college, technical school, culinary arts school, or by earning a four-year college degree. Some learn through apprenticeship programs.[2]

- *Cooks:* The majority of cooks are trained on the job. Many do attend culinary arts school, although it's not a requirement.[3]
- *Culinary arts teachers:* A four-year bachelor's degree is the minimum educational requirement to teach culinary arts. Work experience in the area of teaching is also required, as well as a state-issued certification or license to teach in some cases. These requirements vary by state.[4]

FORMAL TRAINING PROGRAMS: COMMUNITY COLLEGE, UNIVERSITY, AND CULINARY ARTS SCHOOLS

Although in the past, work experience providing on-the-job training was the common track for becoming a chef. In recent years, according to BLS data, formal academic training through community colleges, universities, and specialized culinary art schools has become more common.[5]

These programs provide in-class instruction as well as hands-on kitchen training. Courses offered typically include cooking and baking as well as sanitation and safety, nutrition, and food preparation.

Some aspiring chefs choose to earn certification from programs that run several months. Others pursue a two-year degree at a community college, still others choose a four-year degree from a college or university, and some go on to pursue a master's degree. Which degree is right for you depends on where you want to go in your career, as well as personal factors such as how soon you want to be able to start working full-time versus how much time you want to dedicate to being in school.

> "Even when we have traveled as a family, rented vacation homes everywhere, I cooked. I have always loved to cook for people. So here I am, opening a restaurant."—Ellen Muckstadt, owner of the Wickedpissahchowdah restaurant in southern New Hampshire

WHY CHOOSE AN ASSOCIATE'S DEGREE?

Earning a two-year degree—called an associate's degree—is one way to become qualified to seek work as a chef. You can also choose to use the degree to go further and earn a bachelor's degree. The emphasis of the two-year curriculum is typically on general math skills, writing, English and communication, and, of course, cooking training. This is usually focused on the preparation of fish and meat dishes as well as pastries, and includes Asian, Mediterranean, and American cooking. Menu planning and wine studies are a part of the curriculum as well.

According to CulinarySchools.org, an associate's degree in culinary arts prepares students to:

- Demonstrate expertise in preparing breakfast, lunch, and dinner items using ingredients that are wholesome, sanitary, and nutritious
- Demonstrate baking principles by preparing pastries and sweets
- Manage people within the kitchen
- Select and prepare meat, seafood, and poultry items for service; choose accompaniments for each dish emphasizing different cultures
- Use and care for equipment found in professional kitchens
- Develop an understanding of basic principles of sanitation and safety and ability to apply the sanitation principles of food preparation
- Develop skills in knife, tool, and equipment handling and ability to apply skills in food preparation
- Develop skills in producing a variety of cold food products and buffet designs
- Apply fundamentals of baking and pastry preparation to a variety of products
- Demonstrate an understanding of quality customer service
- Prepare items for buffet presentations, including tallow carvings, bread sculpting, and ice carvings
- Prepare for the transition from employee to supervisor
- Apply principles of menu planning and layout for development of menus in a variety of facilities and service options
- Apply knowledge of laws and regulations relating to safety and sanitation in the commercial kitchen[6]

WHY CHOOSE A BACHELOR'S DEGREE?

A bachelor's degree in the culinary arts—which takes four years to obtain— follows the same general curriculum as an associate's degree but delves deeper into business- and management-related topics. This is because most chefs pursing a bachelor's degree have an interest in a management role at a hotel, restaurant, spa, casino, or any other food-related business. The degree, therefore, offers the same culinary training as an associate's degree, but expands your learning to broaden your career prospects.

Although not required, a bachelor's degree can help you advance your career, give you an edge over the competition in the field, and earn you a higher starting salary than those holding an associate's degree.

Apprenticeship Programs

Potential chefs who do not wish to follow the formal training track can gain knowledge through formal apprenticeships. These provide both hands-on training and classroom education. These apprenticeships are sponsored by many culinary arts schools and food industry organizations, including the American Culinary Federation (ACF).

Voluntary Certification

Chefs who are already working professionally can choose to continue their education via certification programs. The ACF offers many such programs. To be eligible, a participant must have minimal work experience as well as some advanced (post–high school) education.

EDUCATION REQUIREMENTS FOR OTHER CULINARY ARTS CAREERS

While most people associate a career in the culinary arts with being a chef, there are many other types of jobs within the field that require different levels of training and education. As mentioned previously, the educational requirements for jobs in the culinary arts differ according to the career path and role you choose to pursue.

The BLS provides information about education requirements as well as salary and career growth data for all kinds of jobs. The following information is provided by the BLS based on 2017 data.

- *Food scientists:* "Agricultural and food scientists need at least a bachelor's degree from an accredited postsecondary institution, although many get advanced degrees."[7]
- *Food and beverage service managers:* "Most applicants qualify with a high school diploma and several years of work experience in the food service industry. However, some may receive additional training at a community college, technical or vocational school, culinary school, or 4-year college."[8]
- *Dieticians and nutritionists:* "Dietitians and nutritionists typically need a bachelor's degree in dietetics, foods and nutrition, clinical nutrition, public health nutrition, or a related area. Dietitians also may study food service systems management. Programs include courses in nutrition, psychology, chemistry, and biology. Many dietitians and nutritionists have advanced degrees."[9]

THE LIFE OF A BAKER

Mary Ann Quitugua.
*Courtesy of
Mary Ann Quitugua*

Mary Ann Quitugua was born in the Philippines and was raised in Guam, where she grew up in a bakery. She lives in Tacoma, Washington, with her husband, Lance, and their two boys. She is co-owner of Celebrity Cake Studio, a family business that she runs with her sister, Odette. They are a retail and wholesale bakery that specializes in cakes for all occasions, as well as desserts and cookies. They also host fun decorating parties in their facility that empower their customers to create a cake of their own. The tagline for the business is "Where every cake is a work of art!" Mary is responsible for day-to-day operations, managing staff and production, human resources, and sales.

What is a typical day in your job?

I'm a mother of two young boys, so my job starts quite early at home. I have a Slack app that I use to communicate to my staff the expectations of the day. This allows us to be on the same page to reach our daily goals. I check e-mails and will address urgent matters personally; other e-mails will usually be delegated to my front-end staff. After taking care of my kids and dropping them off to school, I am usually at the shop by 10:00 a.m. I meet with our different departments from front-end staff to production crew. During most office days, I am answering e-mails, coordinating production schedules, pallet pickup of large orders, and working on processes. On production days, I will jump in and decorate cakes, teacakes, wedding cakes, and help with the design process. I also consult with clients and take orders as needed.

What's the best part of your job?

The best part of my job is interacting with my staff and customers. I work with the most hard-working and fun-loving team. Our customers are also so lovely, and I make it a point to chat with them and make sure they are happy with our products and services. I also *love* decorating wedding cakes and working on huge cake projects.

What's the worst part of your job?

The worst part of my job is dealing with customers or employees that don't see the value in our business. Since this is a small, family-run business, we take pride in our work, our work environment, and our culture. Dealing with the bureaucracy that comes with owning your own business is no fun as well.

What's the most surprising thing about your job?

I'm always surprised at the new things I learn. It ranges from learning a new design technique, to how our phone systems are programmed and work, to how to troubleshoot situations that don't go as planned.

What's next? Where do you see yourself going from here?

We are launching a new marketing platform for our business that will make it a draw for people looking to be inspired. I see this shifting our engagement with our clients to maximize our collective skills in art, design, creativity, and innovation in all things cake!

Did your education prepare you for the job?

I didn't finish college because we were opening up a new location while I was attending community college. I finished up my semester of working full-time and going to night classes and decided that I would learn by experience. I never regretted that decision and hope to still finish my degree.

Experience-Related Requirements

As mentioned previously, having experience in an actual cooking, baking, serving, business, or other food and beverage service environment will enhance your skills and better prepare you for applying them in actual working situations.

Although attending a cooking school does give you hands-on experience as well as instructional foundation, the expectation for many entering the culinary arts sphere is that some experience-related requirements will be met. The earlier you start, the better—even if you are still in high school or are not ready to pursue a culinary arts degree or complete a culinary arts program.

Considering expanding your real-world experience with an international adventure. The Culinary Institute of America, for example, offers an elective international travel program in which participants can gain exposure to local ingredients, cooking techniques, culinary culture, and authentic cuisine in countries including China, France, Italy, Peru, and Spain.[10]

The following outlines some of the specific training opportunities for various types of culinary arts professionals.

EXPERIENCE REQUIREMENTS FOR CHEFS

If your ambition is to become a head chef in an exclusive restaurant, you are definitely expected to have actual experience not only cooking but also working well with a team in a hectic, often chaotic environment. Typically, a chef is expected to have at least one but up to five years' experience, even if the training begins while you are still in high school. Merely cooking well is not enough.

Having general cooking experience is key, but if you are aiming for a career as a particular type of chef—perhaps a sous chef who prepares sauces—finding a way to work via an apprenticeship of other experience-gaining capacity will be necessary before you can be expected to land a job as a chef.

EXPERIENCE REQUIREMENTS FOR PASTRY CHEFS

Pastry chefs are expected to have the technical skills to prepare anything from elaborate wedding cakes to the most basic of pies. Baking skills and presentation skills—the ability to creatively and attractively produce enticing and attractive pastry treats—are key to making it as a pastry chef, whether you own your own bakery, create wedding cakes to spec, or work in a hotel restaurant. The more experience you have, the greater an edge you will have over your competition and the better your skills will be honed.

Many pastry chefs begin in entry-level roles, assisting a head pastry chef by setting up utensils and keeping the baking space tidy. In addition to learning how to bake, being familiar with a real-world baking environment will give you an edge.

Many pastry chefs gain experience in the following ways:

- *Supermarkets:* Most major supermarket chains have their own bakeries, offering cookies, personalized cakes, and other baked goods to customers. By working in a supermarket bakery, you can expect to gain knowledge of everything from inventory control, merchandising, customer service, and of course baking and decorating.
- *Bakeries:* Be it a small local bakery or a larger corporate one—such as in a hotel, restaurant, or on a cruise ship—working in a bakery will earn you important work experience as well as contacts in the industry.
- *Starting a small business:* Word of mouth in your community can help you gain invaluable experience in taking orders, organizing your time, experimenting with different flavors and designs, and creating customized baked good. This can help you build a portfolio of your work as well as develop a local reputation, even if you are still in your teens.

THERE ARE ALWAYS EXCEPTIONS TO THE RULE!

Although it is definitely true across the culinary arts field that experience require-ments exist for launching a culinary arts career—either through your own initiative or via an internship or elective program offered through a culinary arts school or university program—not everybody follows that track to success.

At the ripe age of eleven, Flynn McGarry began his own supper club from his parent's house. By age sixteen he had launched his own pop-up restaurant in New York City, offering a limited number of guests—twelve was the maximum—to enjoy a fourteen-course tasting menu for the price of $180 a head.

McGarry told *Business Insider* that he was inspired to learn to cook because he wasn't happy with what he, as a young person, was being offered at the table. "I got sick of eating kid food, more or less, and I was very precocious when I was 10 years old. My parents were more than happy to let me take over," he said.[11]

In the spring of 2018, McGarry announced he would open his very first per-manent restaurant in New York City, an establishment that would seat twenty-eight. So with ambition, talent, and a lot of hard work, anything is possible—even in the competitive world of cooking.

REINVENTING THE JEWISH DELI

Zane Caplansky. *Courtesy of Zane Caplansky*

Desperate for a great smoked meat sandwich and unable to find one, Zane Caplansky decided to make his own. That passionate desire was the spark that ignited the Caplansky's Deli phenom-enon ten years ago. What followed was a series of innovations and achievements including: Toronto's first pop-up restaurant, Toronto's first modern food truck, reinventing the traditional Jewish deli, franchising, retail products, and tons of media. Caplansky has been featured on the acclaimed documentary film *Deli Man* as well as more than a dozen TV shows, including CBC's *Dragons' Den* and Food Network's *Diners, Drive-Ins, and Dives* as well as *Guy's Big Project.* He currently hosts

Let's Eat with Zane Caplansky, Canada's most popular weekly food radio show, on Newstalk1010. Caplansky frequently shares his story and ideas for success with corporate audiences across Canada.

What is a typical day in your job?

There is nothing typical in either my day or my "job." Every day is new and different from any other, and that's the way I like it. And being self-employed in the food media world the job is always different, too. In fact, I look at my work as a series of projects that I manage. Let me give you a taste of some of these.

For the last four years I've hosted a weekly food radio show called *Let's Eat with Zane Caplansky*. It's a one-hour show that broadcast live every Saturday at 11:00 a.m. There is also a podcast on iheartradio.ca. The show is a constant source of joy. It has allowed me to connect with people I've admired and introduced me to the most fascinating people I likely would not have met otherwise.

What's the most surprising thing about your job?

Doing a live radio show is exhilarating. More than once I've had guests cancel their appearances moments before going on air. Imagine that red light coming on, knowing tens of thousands of people are listening, and you have no guest and the show you'd planned is off the rails. But it always works out. My listeners love to text and call so on those shows I'll turn to them for support.

I produce the show myself. That means I research and book guests, work with sponsors, attend food industry events and listen to pitches from people who want to come on the show, and engage with listeners to better understand what they want to hear on the show.

I do quite a lot of food festival hosting, public appearances, and speaking to corporate groups, associations, and students. I love this stuff because it's so richly experiential. Being with people makes me happy, and being with people and food is even better. Getting a chance to share my stories, to inspire others is a humbling opportunity.

What's the best part of your job?

The best part is that it feels like I'm driving this bus. The restaurant business never felt that way. Now, I decide how busy I want to be, which projects to take on and which to pass up. I'm working on a book about my experiences and hope to have that finished next year. It's been a wild ride and I'm excited to see what happens around the next corner.

What's been a difficult aspect of your job?

At age forty, after many years working in various aspects of the restaurant/hospitality industry, I opened Caplansky's Delicatessen in 2008. It started as a pop-up but evolved into a thriving restaurant in downtown Toronto, a food truck, a catering business, a line of mustards in grocery stores, and then we opened a few franchises. The food truck was a media magnet and brought me to the attention of Food Network. I appeared on various shows, including Guy Fieri's *Diners, Drive-Ins, and Dives*, and worked as a judge or principal character on six seasons of three different Food Network shows in Canada and the United States.

After almost ten years in business, I closed our downtown location due to a dispute with our landlord. It was a tough decision, but it's worked out for the best. After years of stress and struggling with an unreasonable landlord, I closed the doors and walked away.

At first, it was devastating for me. So much of my identity and daily activity was tied to working in the deli. I loved the hustle and bustle. The staff were amazing, but my favorite thing was watching people enjoy my food and giving them the best deli experience possible. Even better? When people would choose to celebrate with us: birthdays, anniversaries, reunions, and so much more. We even had a couple exchange vows in the deli. Now that wouldn't happen anymore.

Slowly the dark clouds began to clear and I realized that a new day had begun. My radio show was a welcome constant. I also started to produce a food-related web series. My work hosting food festivals is more fun than work. My franchise restaurant is doing great and I spend a lot of time there.

What kind of training did you complete to prepare for your job?

I first learned to cook in university living with my brother. Mark taught me some basics like tomato sauce and sauces braised with canned cream of mushroom soup sauce.

After that there was a lot of trial and error. I love cookbooks and tried making recipes I found. When I started working in restaurants, I'd always get the chefs to teach me techniques and dishes. After becoming an apprentice chef, I attended college for culinary management. But I'm still learning.

What's next? Where do you see yourself going from here?

As well as my show, I've turned my focus to my line of deli products in grocery stores. The consumer packaged goods business presents a huge opportunity and is much less stressful than the restaurant ever was. My mustards are back in production, as are my cured smoked meat briskets, corned beef, salami, burgers, smoked turkey, hot dogs, bagels, and more.

Teaching is a new project, but I love it. Centennial College has hired me to teach their Food Tourism and Food Media courses. As a young(ish) apprentice chef, I attended a similar college program and loved that education. Now, it feels like I'm "paying it forward": passing along the wisdom and experience that I've gained in over twenty years working in this industry.

======

Summary

This chapter covered a lot of ground in terms of how to tackle the challenge of not only discovering what career within the culinary arts is right for you and in what environment, capacity, and work culture you want to work, but also how best to prepare yourself for achieving your career goal.

In this chapter, you learned about the broad range of roles that fall under the career umbrella of the culinary arts. And while the various subcareers that exist—from pastry chef to beverage manager—the chapter also pointed to many tools and methods that can help you navigate the confusing path to choosing a career that is right for you. It also addressed some of the specific training and educational options and requirements and expectations that will put you, no matter what your current education level or age, at a strong advantage in a competitive field.

Use this chapter as a guideline for how to best discover what type of career will be the right fit for you and consider what steps you can already be taking to get there. Some tips to remember:

- With all the choices available to you within the culinary arts, take time to consider what kind of work environment you see yourself working in, and what kind of schedule, interaction with colleagues, work culture, and responsibilities you want to have.
- Many culinary arts careers require hours of on-site, on-the-job training. If you have already graduated from high school, consider doing an apprenticeship to gain the training and work experience you need to succeed in your career.

- Learn as much as you can about the different types of jobs available in the culinary arts field. Shadow a culinary arts professional to get a feeling for what hours they keep, what challenges they face, and what the overall job entails. Talk with professionals in your neighborhood—deli workers, chefs, line cooks, bakers, and caterers, for example—to learn what they love about their job, what challenges they face, and what education or training they completed before launching their careers.
- Investigate various colleges, culinary arts schools, and apprenticeship opportunities so you can better prepare yourself for the next step in your career path.
- Don't feel you have to wait until you graduate from high school to begin taking steps to accomplish your career goals. Consider working in a restaurant or volunteering in a meal center. And, of course, practice your skills by cooking and baking when you can.
- Keep work-life balance in mind. The career you choose will be one of many adult decisions you make, and ensuring that you keep all of your priorities—family, location, work schedule—in mind will help you choose the right career for you, which will make you a happier person.

Chapter 3 will go into detail about the next steps—writing a résumé and cover letter, interviewing well, follow-up communications, and more. This is information you can use to secure internships, volunteer positions, summer jobs, and more. It's not just for college grads. In fact, the sooner you can hone these communication skills, the better off you'll be in the professional world.

Pursuing the Educational Path

*M*aking decisions about your career can feel difficult enough without adding to it the process of choosing the educational path that is best for you. This is a decision that demands understanding about not only what kind of education or training is required for the career you want but also what kind of school or college you want to attend. There is a lot to consider no matter what area of study you want to pursue, but with the culinary arts it can be even more complicated because, as discussed in chapter 2, various careers within the culinary arts field require different levels of education and training.

Now that you've gotten an overview of the different degree, certificate, and on-the-job training options that can prepare you for your future career, this chapter will dig more deeply into how to best choose the right type of study for you. Even if you are years away from earning your high school diploma or equivalent, it's never too soon to start weighing your options, thinking about the application process, and of course taking time to really consider what kind of educational track and environment will suit you best.

Some people choose to start their careers right away, with apprenticeship programs or on-the-job training. Not everyone wants to take time to go to college or pursue other forms of academic-based training. But if you are interested in following the educational path—from earning a certificate in culinary arts to a four-year university degree—this chapter will help you navigate the process of deciding on the type of institution you would most thrive in, determining what type of degree you want to earn, and looking into costs and how to find help in meeting them.

The chapter will also give you advice on the application process; how to prepare for entrance exams you may need to take, such as the SAT or ACT; and how to communicate your passion, ambition, and personal experience in a personal statement. When you've completed this chapter, you should have a good sense of what kind of post–high school education is right for you and how to ensure you have the best chance of being accepted at the institution of your choice.

> "I have a bachelor's degree in journalism and a master's degree in social work. It seems a little strange, but I would say that both have contributed to why I consider the two businesses I've started a success."—Christopher Collins, founder of Lucky Louie's Sausage and Hot Dogs

Finding a Program or School That Fits Your Personality

Before getting into the details of good schools for each profession, it's a good idea for you to take some time to consider what type of school will be best for you. Just as with your future work environment, understanding how you best learn, what type of atmosphere best fits your personality, and how and where you are most likely to succeed will play a major part in how happy you will be with your choice. This section will provide some thinking points to help you refine what kind of school or program is the best fit for you.

Note that this list does not assume you intend to attend a four-year college program or complete a certification program—some of the questions may therefore be more or less relevant to you, depending on the path of study you plan to follow.

If nothing else, answering questions like the following ones can help you narrow your search and focus on a smaller sampling of choices. Write your answers to these questions down somewhere where you can refer to them often, such as in your notes app on your phone:

- *Size*: Does the size of the school matter to you? Colleges and universities range in size from five hundred or fewer students to twenty-five thousand students. If you are considering culinary arts schools, think about what size class you would like and what the right instructor-to-student ratio is for you.

- *Community location:* Would you prefer to be in a rural area, a small town, a suburban area, or a large city? How important is the location of the school in the larger world? Is the flexibility of an online degree or certification program attractive to you, or do you prefer more on-site, hands-on instruction?

- *Length of study:* How many months or years do you want to put into your education before you start working professionally?

- *Housing options:* If applicable, what kind of housing would you prefer? Dorms, off-campus apartments, and private homes are all common options.

- *Student body:* How would you like the student body to look? Think about coed versus all-male and all-female settings, as well as ethnic and racial diversity, how many students are part-time versus full-time, and the percentage of commuter students.

- *Academic environment:* Which majors are offered, and at which degree levels? Research the student-faculty ratio. Are the classes taught often by actual professors or more often by the teaching assistants? How many internships does the school typically provide to students? Are independent study or study abroad programs available in your area of interest?

- *Financial aid availability/cost:* Does the school provide ample opportunities for scholarships, grants, work-study programs, and the like? Does cost play a role in your options? (For most people, it does.)

- *Support services:* How strong are the school's academic and career placement counseling services?

- *Social activities and athletics:* Does the school offer clubs that you are interested in? Which sports are offered? Are scholarships available?

- *Specialized programs:* Does the school offer honors programs or programs for veterans or students with disabilities or special needs?

Not all of these questions are going to be important to you, and that's fine. Be sure to make note of aspects that don't matter as much to you. You might change your mind as you visit colleges, but it's important to make note of where you are to begin with.

U.S. News & World Report puts it best when it reports that what fits you best—and this applies to culinary art schools and certificate programs as well—is one that:

- Offers a degree that matches your interests and needs
- Provides a style of instruction that matches the way you like to learn
- Provides a level of academic rigor to match your aptitude and preparation
- Offers a community that feels like home to you
- Values you for what you do well[1]

MAKE THE MOST OF CAMPUS VISITS

If it's at all practical and feasible, you should visit the campuses of all the schools you're considering. To get a real feel for any college or university, you need to walk around the campus, spend some time in the common areas where students hang out, and sit in on a few classes. You can also sign up for campus tours, which are typically given by current students. This is another good way to see the campus and ask questions of someone who knows. Be sure to visit the specific school/building that covers your intended major as well. Websites and brochures won't be able to convey that intangible feeling you'll get from a visit.

Make a list of questions that are important to you before you visit. In addition to the questions listed in the earlier section "Finding a College That Fits Your Personality," consider these questions as well:

- What is the makeup of the current freshman class? Is the campus diverse?
- What is the meal plan like? What are the food options?
- Where do most of the students hang out between classes? (Be sure to visit this area.)
- How long does it take to walk from one end of campus to the other?
- What types of transportation are available for students? Does campus security provide escorts to cars, dorms, and other on-campus destinations at night?

To prepare for your visit and make the most of it, consider these tips and words of advice:

- Be sure to do some research. At the very least, spend some time on the college's website. You may find your questions are addressed adequately there.
- Make a list of questions.
- Arrange to meet with a professor in your area of interest or to visit the specific school.
- Be prepared to answer questions about yourself and why you are interested in this school.
- Dress in neat, clean, and casual clothes. Avoid overly wrinkled clothing or anything with stains.
- Listen and take notes.
- Don't interrupt.
- Be positive and energetic.
- Make eye contact when someone speaks directly to you.
- Ask questions.
- Thank people for their time.

Finally, be sure to send thank-you notes or e-mails after the visit is over. Remind recipients when you visited the campus and thank them for their time.

Hopefully, this section has impressed upon you the importance of finding the right fit for your chosen learning institution. Take some time to paint a mental picture of the kind of university or school setting that will best complement your needs.

HOW IMPORTANT IS ACCREDITATION?

In the world of the culinary arts, as with other academic fields of study, accreditation matters, and it is something you should consider when choosing a school. Accreditation is basically a seal of approval that assures prospective students that the institution will provide a quality education that is worth the investment and will help graduates reach their career goals. However, not all accreditation is equal, and some, according to the website the Reluctant Gourmet, "mean little more than that the school pays an annual fee to an 'Accreditation Body' that comes up with its own guidelines and qualifications that may or may not be important."[2]

Be sure you understand what a school's particular accreditation actually means. The top professional chefs' organization in the United States, the American Culinary Federation (www.acfchefs.org), grants accreditation to culinary schools only after a thorough evaluation of the curriculum, facilities, ratio of students to instructors, certification of instructors, and other factors. A school that is ACF-accredited is one you can feel sure will offer a quality education that will be recognized by future employers.

Determining Your Education Plan

As discussed earlier, there are many options when it comes to pursing an education in the culinary arts. These include vocational schools, two-year community colleges, four-year colleges, or culinary arts schools. This section will help you select the track that is best suited to you.

Online programs are especially worth considering for careers in the culinary arts that do not require hands-on training in a kitchen, such as culinary operations and hospitality management. These programs can be completed without ever stepping foot in a classroom.

Whether you are opting for a certificate program, a two-year, or four-year degree, you will find there are many choices of institutes and schools that offer a variety of programs at different costs and durations. (In the case of certificate programs, twelve to eighteen months is usually the average for full-time participants to complete the required course load.) Because of this, it is important to narrow down the options and compare them closely.

It's a good idea to select roughly five to ten schools in a realistic location (for you) that offer the degree or certification you want to earn. If you are considering online programs, include these in your list. Of course, not every school near you or that you have an initial interest in will offer the degree you

CONSIDERING A GAP YEAR

Taking a year off between high school and college, often called a gap year, is normal, perfectly acceptable, and almost required in many countries around the world. It is becoming increasingly acceptable in the United States as well. Because the cost of college has gone up dramatically, it literally pays for you to know going in what you want to study, and a gap year—well spent—can do lots to help you answer that question. It can also give you an opportunity to explore different types of culinary-related jobs to help you find a deeper sense of what you'd like to study when your gap year has ended.

Some great ways to spend your gap year include joining organizations such as Peace Corps or AmeriCorps, both of which offer opportunities for cooking and cooking-related work.[3] But even if the experience has nothing to do directly with cooking, a gap year can help you see things from a new perspective. Consider enrolling in a mountaineering program or other gap year–styled program, backpacking across Europe or other countries on the cheap (be safe and bring a friend), finding a volunteer organization that furthers a cause you believe in or that complements your career aspirations, joining a Road Scholar program (see www.roadscholar.org), teach English in another country (more information is available at www.gooverseas.com/blog/best-countries-for-seniors-to-teach-english-abroad), or work and earn money for college!

Many students will find that they get much more out of college when they have a year to mature and to experience the real world. The American Gap Year Association reports from alumni surveys that students who take gap years show greater civic engagement, higher college graduation rates, and higher grade point averages (GPAs) in college.

One caveat, though: If you aren't highly motivated to attend college, it can be somewhat dangerous to take a year off. Some kids tend to never return to school once they're away from it for a year. Be sure you have a plan and can stick to it if you're taking a year off.

See the association's website at https://gapyearassociation.org for lots of advice and resources if you're considering this potentially life-altering experience.

want, so narrow your choices accordingly. With that said, consider attending a public college or university in your resident state, if possible, which will save you lots of money. Private institutions don't typically discount resident student tuition costs.

Be sure you research the basic GPA and SAT or ACT requirements of each school as well. Although some community colleges do not require standardized tests for the application process, others do.

If you are planning to apply to a college or program that requires the ACT or SAT, advisers recommend that students take both the ACT and the SAT tests during the spring of their junior year at the latest. You can retake these tests and use your highest score, so be sure to leave time for a retake early in your senior year if needed. You want your best score to be available to all the schools you're applying to by January of your senior year, which will also enable your score to be considered with any scholarship applications. Keep in mind that these are general timelines—be sure to check the exact deadlines and calendars of the schools to which you're applying!

Once you have found five to ten schools in a realistic location for you that offer the degree or certification you want to pursue, spend some time on their websites studying the requirements for admission. Important factors in your decision about what schools to apply to should include whether or not you meet the requirements, your chances of getting in (but shoot high!), tuition costs and availability of scholarships and grants, location, and the school's reputation and licensure/graduation rates.

Most colleges and universities will list the average stats for the last class accepted to the program, which will give you a sense about your chances of acceptance.

The importance of these characteristics will depend on your grades and test scores, your financial resources, your work experience, and other personal factors. Taking everything into account, you should be able to narrow your list down to the schools that best match your educational and professional goals as well as your resources and other factors such as location and duration of study.

What's It Going to Cost You?

So, the bottom line: what will your education end up costing you? Of course, this depends on many factors, including the type and length of degree or certification you pursue, where you attend (in-state or not, private or public institution), how much in scholarships or financial aid you're able to obtain, your family or personal income, and many other factors. This section will provide information on costs for the various types of programs and institutions that provide education in the culinary arts.

A culinary arts certificate or diploma program averages between $17,550 and $47,000. In comparison, a two-year degree averages $35,000 between $56,000, and a four-year degree between $47,000 and $120,000, according to the website CostHelper.com.[4]

School can be an expensive investment, but there are many ways to seek help paying for your education. © *iStock/Getty Images Plus/Photobuay*

Keep in mind that these are averages. If you read more specific data about a particular university or find averages in your particular area of interest, you should assume those numbers are closer to reality than these, as they are more specific. This data helps to show you the ballpark figures.

Generally speaking, there is about a 3 percent annual increase in tuition and associated costs to attend college. In other words, if you are expecting to attend college two years after this data was collected, you need to add approximately 6 percent to these numbers. Keep in mind that this assumes there are no financial aid or scholarships of any kind.

WRITING A GREAT PERSONAL STATEMENT FOR ADMISSION

The personal statement you include with your application to college is extremely important, especially if your GPA and SAT/ACT scores are on the border of what is typically accepted. Write something that is thoughtful and conveys your understanding of the profession you are interested in, as well as your desire to practice in this field. Why are you uniquely qualified? Why are you a good fit for the program to which you are applying? These essays should be highly personal (the "personal" in personal statement). Will the admissions professionals who read it—along with hundreds of others—come away with a snapshot of who you really are and what you are passionate about?

Look online for some examples of good personal statements, which will give you a feel for what works. Be sure to check your specific school for length guidelines, format requirements, and any other guidelines they expect you to follow.

And of course, be sure to proofread it several times and ask a professional (such as your school writing center or your local library services) to proofread it as well.

Financial Aid: Finding Money for Education

Finding the money to attend college—whether a two- or four-years college program, an online program, or a vocational career college—can seem overwhelming. But you can do it if you have a plan before you actually start applying to colleges. If you get into your top-choice university, don't let the sticker price turn you away. Financial aid can come from many different sources, and it's available to cover all different kinds of costs you'll encounter during your years in college, including tuition, fees, books, housing, and food.

The good news is that universities more often offer incentive or tuition discount aid to encourage students to attend. The market is often more competitive in the favor of the student, and colleges and universities are responding by offering more generous aid packages to a wider range of students than they used to. Here are some basic tips and pointers about the financial aid process:

- Apply for financial aid during your senior year. You must fill out the Free Application for Federal Student Aid (FAFSA) form, which can be filed starting October 1 of your senior year until June of the year you graduate.[5] Because the amount of available aid is limited, it's best to apply as soon as you possibly can. See https://studentaid.cd.gov/sa/fafsa to get started.
- Be sure to compare and contrast the deals you get from different schools. There is room to negotiate with universities. The first offer for aid may not be the best you'll get.
- Wait until you receive all offers from your top schools and then use this information to negotiate with your top choice to see if they will match or beat the best aid package you received.
- To be eligible to keep and maintain your financial aid package, you must meet certain grade/GPA requirements. Be sure you are very clear about these academic expectations and keep up with them.
- You must reapply for federal aid every year.

Watch out for scholarship scams! You should never be asked to pay to submit the FAFSA form (*free* is in its name) or be required to pay a lot to find appropriate aid and scholarships. These are free services. If an organization promises you you'll get aid or that you have to "act now or miss out," these are warning signs of a less-than-reputable organization.

You should also be careful with your personal information to avoid identity theft as well. Simple things like closing and exiting your browser after visiting sites where you entered personal information goes a long way. Don't share your student aid ID number with anyone either.

It's important to understand the different forms of financial aid that are available to you. That way, you'll know how to apply for different kinds and get the best financial aid package that fits your needs and strengths. The two main categories that financial aid falls under are gift aid, which doesn't have to be repaid, and self-help aid, which includes loans that must be repaid and work-study funds that are earned. The next sections cover the various types of financial aid that fit into these areas.

GRANTS

Grants typically are awarded to students who have financial need, but can also be used in the areas of athletics, academics, demographics, veteran support, and special talents. They do not have to be paid back. Grants can come from federal agencies, state agencies, specific universities, and private organizations. Most federal and state grants are based on financial need.

Examples of grants are the Pell Grant, SMART Grant, and the Federal Supplemental Educational Opportunity Grant (FSEOG). Visit the US Department of Education's Federal Student Aid site at https://studentaid.ed .gov/types/grands-scholarships for lots of current information about grants.

SCHOLARSHIPS

Scholarships are merit-based aid that does not have to be paid back. They are typically awarded based on academic excellence or some other special talent, such as music or art. Scholarships can also be athletic-based, minority-based, aid for women, and so forth. These are typically not awarded by federal or state governments, but instead come from the specific university you applied to as well as private and nonprofit organizations.

Be sure to reach out directly to the financial aid officers of the schools you want to attend. These people are great contacts who can lead you to many more sources of scholarships and financial aid. Visit GoCollege's Financial Aid Finder at www.gocollege.com/financial-aid/scholarships/types for lots more informa-tion about how scholarships in general work.

LOANS

Many types of loans are available especially for students to pay for their postsec-ondary education. However, the important thing to remember here is that loans must be paid back, with interest. (This is the extra cost of borrowing the money and is usually a percentage of the amount you borrow.) Be sure you understand the interest rate you will be charged. Is this fixed or will it change over time? Are payments on the loan and interest deferred until you graduate (meaning you don't have to begin paying it off until after you graduate)? Is the loan subsidized (meaning the federal government pays the interest until you graduate)? These are all points you need to be clear about before you sign on the dotted line.

There are many types of loans offered to students, including need-based loans, non-need-based loans, state loans, and private loans. Two very reputable federal loans are the Perkins Loan and the Direct Stafford Loan. For more information about student loans, visit https://bigfuture.collegeboard.org/pay-for-college/loans/types-of-college-loans.

FEDERAL WORK-STUDY

The US federal work-study program provides part-time jobs for undergraduate and graduate students with financial need so they can earn money to pay for educational expenses. The focus of such work is on community service work and work related to a student's course of study. Not all colleges and universities participate in this program, so be sure to check with the financial aid office at any schools you are considering if this is something you are counting on. The sooner you apply, the more likely you will get the job you desire and be able to benefit from the program, as funds are limited. See https://studentaid.ed.gov/sa/types/work-study for more information about this opportunity.

PAIRING A LOVE OF PUBLISHING WITH A PASSION FOR COOKING

Kim Laidlaw.
Courtesy of Kim Laidlaw

Kim Laidlaw, owner of Cast Iron Media, LLC, is an award-winning cookbook editor, producer, and the author of five cookbooks: *Williams Sonoma Everyday Slow Cooking, Quick Slow Cooking, Home Baked Comfort,* IACP award–nominated *Baby & Toddler on the Go,* and *Dessert of the Day.* With more than seventeen years of experience in cookbook publishing and packaging, Laidlaw has managed hundreds of projects from conception to completion. Her clients include Weber Grills, Kendall-Jackson Winery, Williams Sonoma, KitchenAid, Morton Salt, *Saveur*, *EatingWell*, *Sunset*, KQED Inc., CBSinteractive/CHOW.com, American Girl, BabyCenter, and more. She has worked with countless publishers, and as executive editor at Weldon Owen Publishing for more than eleven years has packaged and managed more than one hundred cookbooks, many of which were branded Williams Sonoma. Laidlaw is also a recipe developer and tester for such clients as Morton Salt, KitchenAid, Mary's Pizza Shack, Food Network star Tanya Holland, CHOW.com, KQED Inc., and many other chefs, bloggers, and cookbook authors. She is a former instructor at the acclaimed San Francisco Cooking School. She graduated from the California Culinary Academy and previously worked as a professional baker at La Farine French Bakery in Oakland, California.

What is a typical day in your job?

There is no typical day in my job. I wear a lot of hats: cookbook producer, cookbook author, editor, writer, recipe developer and tester. I've also taught baking classes, been a food stylist, and even a hand model. Primarily though, I'm in one of three places: Either at my desk on my computer, where I am working with my author, client, or creative team to put together a book (from concept to completion); on a photo set with my photography team (or planning a photo shoot); or in the kitchen researching, testing, and writing recipes. I also spend a fair amount of time at the grocery store when I'm in the midst of a recipe development project.

What's the best part of your job?

I love the diversity of it. When I first went freelance I tried all sorts of different jobs in the food world: teaching, food styling, etc. But I've mostly reined it in as producing and project managing cookbooks, occasionally writing one, and doing recipe development and testing. I love that I can both manage a project, but still also be in the kitchen. In my work I feel like I have a great balance of being creative, working with creative people, and bringing structure to a project. I also love that I have my own business, so I'm not stuck in meetings all day like I was when I worked as an executive editor at a publishing company. Finally, I love coming up with new recipe ideas and being able to execute them successfully.

What's the worst part of your job?

Being a freelancer brings its own set of issues—like where my next job or project is going to come from. That is probably the hardest part. You are only as good as your last job with a client, so if something goes wrong (whether or not it's your fault), you might not be hired again. You also have to hustle and put yourself out there. I'm not super excited about doing that. I've been fortunate that most clients have come to me, as I've been in the industry now for sixteen-plus years.

What's the most surprising thing about your job?

That I get paid to make books about food! For example, I find it a bit hilarious when we are on a photo shoot (which I project manage) and we are taking a picture of, say, a hamburger, and it has to look just right. And the number of people it takes to organize that photo shoot, make the food, style the food and the props, and take the photo. I'm just hoping that people continue to want physical cookbooks. It's one of the last book frontiers.

What's next? Where do you see yourself going from here?

I'd love to keep doing what I'm doing, but I see the industry changing. I think moving into more online content and working more closely with brands. That's pretty much what I specialize in now, national and international brands. I've worked with Williams Sonoma, American Girl, Weber, KitchenAid, Kendall-Jackson, and more. I actually enjoy working with brands in this capacity, it helps tell their story in a more personalized way. And if I can inject decent, quality food into the mix all the better.

Did your education prepare you for the job?

Yes, I think so. I have a BA in communications with a minor in the arts, plus I went to culinary school for baking and pastry and worked as a professional baker for a time.

Is the job what you expected?

Nope. I think when I was in my late twenties working in the computer book publishing business, I dreamed of doing cookbooks. I never actually thought I could make it happen. Now, many years later, I know it backward and forward, but it's constantly changing; new challenges arise, and new clients bring their own complications and identities and insights. And I hope to continue to grow with the industry to see where it will take me.

Summary

This chapter covered all the aspects of college and postsecondary schooling/certification that you'll want to consider as you move forward. Remember that finding the right fit is especially important, as it increases the chances that you'll stay in school and earn your degree or certificate—and have an amazing experience while you're at it. The careers covered in this book have varying educational requirements, which means that finding the right school or program can be very different depending on your career aspirations.

In this chapter, you learned how to evaluate and compare your options in order to get the best education for the best deal. You also learned a little about scholarships and financial aid, how the SAT and ACT tests work, if applicable, and how to write a unique personal statement that eloquently expresses your passions.

Use this chapter as a jumping-off point to dig deeper into your particular area of interest, but don't forget these important points:

- Take the SAT and ACT tests early in your junior year so you have time to take them again if you need to. Most universities automatically accept the highest scores.
- Make sure that the institution you plan to attend has an accredited program in your field of study.
- Don't underestimate how important campus visits are, especially in the pursuit of finding the right academic fit. Come prepared to ask questions not addressed on the school's website or in the literature.
- Your personal statement is a very important piece of your application that can set you apart from other applicants. Take the time and energy needed to make it unique and compelling.
- Don't assume you can't afford a school based on the sticker price. Many schools offer great scholarships and aid to qualified students. It doesn't hurt to apply. This advice especially applies to minorities, veterans, and students with disabilities.
- Don't lose sight of the fact that it's important to pursue a career that you enjoy, are good at, and are passionate about! You'll be a happier person if you do so.

At this point, your career goals and aspirations should be jelling. At the very least, you should have a plan for finding out more information. And don't forget about networking. Remember to do the research about the university, school, or degree/certificate program before you reach out and especially before you visit. Faculty and staff find students who ask challenging questions much more impressive than those who ask questions that can be answered by spending ten minutes on the school's website.

Chapter 4 goes into detail about the next steps—writing a résumé and cover letter, interviewing well, follow-up communications, and more. This information is not jut for college grads; you can use it to secure internships, volunteer positions, summer jobs, and other opportunities. In fact, the sooner you can hone these communication skills, the better off you'll be in the professional world.

4

Writing Your Résumé and Interviewing

You are now well on your way to mapping a path to achieve your career goals in the culinary arts field. Each chapter of this book has narrowed the process from the broadest of strokes—what is the culinary arts and what kinds of jobs exist in it—to how to plan your strategy and educational approach to making your dream job a reality.

This chapter will cover the steps involved in applying for jobs or schools: how to prepare an effective résumé and slam dunk an interview. Your résumé is your opportunity to summarize your experience, training, education, and goals and attract employers or school administrators. The goal of the résumé is to land the interview, and the goal of the interview is to land the job. Even if you do not have much working experience, you can still put together a résumé that expresses your interests and goals and the activities that illustrate your competence and interest.

As well as a résumé, you will be expected to write a cover letter that is basically your opportunity to reveal a little bit more about your passion and your motivation for a particular job or educational opportunity, and often to express more about you personally to give a potential employer a sense of who you are and what drives you.

Giving the right impression is undoubtedly important, but don't let that make you nervous. In a résumé, cover letter, or interview, you want to put forward your best but your genuine self. Dress professionally and proofread carefully, but ensure you are being yourself. This chapter will discuss all of these important aspects of the job-hunting process, and by the end you will feel confident and ready to present yourself as a candidate for the job you really want.

When looking for samples of résumé content and design, be as specific to the type of job you want as possible. For example, the Branford Hall career institute offers samples of résumés aimed at jobs in the culinary arts.[1] Melissa King at the website The Nest offers more tips for how to prepare a winning culinary arts résumé.[2]

Writing Your Résumé

Writing your first résumé can feel very challenging because you have likely not yet gained a lot of experience in a professional setting. But don't fret: Employers understand that you are new to the workforce or to the particular career you are seeking. The right approach is never to exaggerate or invent experience or accomplishments, but to present yourself as someone with a good work ethic and a genuine interest in the particular job or company, and use what you can to present yourself authentically and honestly.

Before you even begin to write your résumé, do your research. Make sure you get a good sense of what kind of candidate or applicant a school or an employer is looking for. You want to not only come across as competent and qualified, you want to seem like just the right fit for just that job within that organization.

Once you know more about the intended audience—organization, institution, or individual—of your résumé, you can begin to make a list of all the relevant experience and education you have. You may need to customize your résumé for different purposes to ensure you are not filling it with information that does not directly link to your qualifications for a particular job.

Highlight your education where you can—any courses you've taken, be it in high school or through a community college or any other place that offers training related to your job target. Also highlight any hobbies or volunteer experience you have—but again, only as it relates to the job you are after.

"There is no typical day in my job. I wear a lot of hats: cookbook producer, cookbook author, editor, writer, recipe developer and tester. I've also taught baking classes, been a food stylist, and even a hand model."—Kim Laidlaw, cookbook author and editor

Your résumé is a document that sums up who you are and indicates the ways you will be an asset to your future employer. But the trick is it should also be concise: one page is usually appropriate, especially for your very first résumé.

Before preparing your résumé, try to connect with a hiring professional—a human resources person or hiring manager—in a position or organization similar to the one you are interested in. He or she can give you advice on what employers look for and what information to highlight on your résumé, as well as what types of interview questions you can expect.

As important as your résumé's content is the way you design and format it. You can find several samples online of résumés that you can be inspired by. At The Balance Careers, for example, you can find many templates and design ideas.[3]

You want your résumé to be attractive to the eye and formatted in a way that makes the key points easy to spot and digest—according to some research, employees take an average of six seconds to review a résumé, so you don't have a lot of time to get across your experience and value.

There are some standard elements to an effective résumé that you should be sure to include. At the top should be your name, of course, as well as your e-mail address and other contact information. Always list your experience in chronological order, beginning with your current or most recent position— or whatever experience you want to share. If you are a recent graduate with little work experience, begin with your education. If you've been in the working world for a while, you can opt to list your education or any certifications you have earned at the bottom. The important thing is to present the most important and relevant information at the top. With only six seconds to make an impression, your résumé needs to be easy to navigate and read.

Your headline will appear just below your name and should summarize—in 120 characters—who you are, what you do, what you are interested in doing, and what motivates you. Take your time with this—it is your opportunity to sell yourself in a brief and impactful manner. Related but separate is your summary section. Here, you can share a little more about yourself than in your headline, but it should still be brief. Waldman recommends your summary take no more than thirty seconds to read aloud (so yes, time yourself!); that it be short (between five and ten lines or three to five sentences), concise, and unique; and that it tell a story.

LINKING-IN WITH IMPACT

As well as your paper or electronic résumé, creating a LinkedIn profile is a good way to highlight your experience and promote yourself, as well as to network. Joining professional organizations and connecting with other people in your desired field are good ways to keep abreast of changes and trends and work opportunities.

The key elements of a LinkedIn profile are your photo, your headline, and your profile summary. These are the most revealing parts of the profile and the ones employers and connections will use to form their impression of you.

The photo should be carefully chosen. Remember that LinkedIn is not Facebook or Instagram: It is not the place to share a photo of you acting too casually on vacation or at a party. According to Joshua Waldman, author of *Job Searching with Social Media for Dummies*, the choice of photo should be taken seriously and be done right. His tips:

- Choose a photo in which you have a nice smile.
- Dress in professional clothing.
- Ensure the background of the photo is pleasing to the eye. According to Waldman, some colors—like green and blue—convey a feeling of trust and stability.
- Remember it's not a mug shot. You can be creative with the angle of your photo rather than staring directly into the camera.
- Use your photo to convey some aspect of your personality. If you are looking for a job in the culinary arts, consider a photo that expresses your love of cooking.
- Focus on your face. Remember, visitors to your profile will see only a small thumbnail image, so be sure your face takes up most of it.[4]

"The best part of my job is interacting with my staff and customers. I work with the most hard-working and fun-loving team. Our customers are also so lovely, and I make it a point to chat with them and make sure they are happy with our products and services."—Mary Ann Quitugua, baker

Writing Your Cover Letter

In addition to your résumé, most employers will ask you to submit a cover letter. This is a one-page letter in which you express your motivation, why you are interested in the organization or position, and what skills you possess that make you the right fit.

Here are some tips for writing an effective cover letter:

- As always, proofread your text carefully before submitting it.
- Be sure you have a letter that is focused on a specific job. Do not make it too general or one-size-fits-all.
- Summarize why you are right for the position.
- Keep your letter to one page.
- Introduce yourself in a way that makes the reader want to know more about you and encourages them to review your résumé.
- Be specific about the job you are applying for. Mention the job title and be sure it is correct.
- Try to find the name of the person who will receive your letter rather than using the nonspecific "To Whom It May Concern."
- Be sure you include your contact details.
- End with a call to action—a request for an interview, for example.

Interviewing Skills

With your sparkling résumé and LinkedIn profile, you are bound to be called for an interview. This is an important stage to reach: You will have already gone through several filters—a potential employer has gotten a quick scan of your experience (remember, on average a résumé is viewed for only six seconds!) and has reviewed your LinkedIn profile and has made the decision to learn more about you in person.

There's no way to know ahead of time exactly what to expect in an interview, but there are many ways to prepare yourself. You can start by learning more about the person who will be interviewing you. In the same way recruiters and employers can learn about you online, you can do the same. You can see if you have any education or work experience in common, or any contacts you both know.

A job interview can be stressful, but with the right preparation you will interview with confidence. © *iStock/Getty Images Plus/FlamingoImages*

Preparing yourself for the types of questions you will be asked to ensure you offer a thoughtful and meaningful response is vital to interview success. Consider your answers carefully, and be prepared to support them with examples and anecdotes.

At The Balance Careers, you can find questions particular to an interview for a job within the culinary arts. Some examples include:

- Why did you decide to become a chef? What other back-of-the-house positions have you previously held?
- Did you go to culinary school? What credentials did you earn through your culinary studies?
- What did you like best about the education experience? What did you like least?
- Where and how were you trained?
- What is your management style? What management style do you prefer for your supervisor to have?
- Are you a team player? Describe your usual role in a team-centered work environment? Do you easily assume a leadership role?
- Do you have a sense of humor?[5]

After the interview, it is a good idea to follow up with a message to the interviewer thanking them for their time and reiterating your interest in the company and position. This is traditionally done with a letter, but an e-mail is just as appropriate.

BEWARE WHAT YOU SHARE ON SOCIAL MEDIA

Most of us engage in social media. Sites such as Facebook, Twitter, and Instagram provide us a platform for sharing photos and memories, opinions and life events, and reveal everything from our political stance to our sense of humor. It's a great way to connect with people around the world, but once you post something, it's accessible to anyone—including potential employers—unless you take mindful precaution.

Your posts may be public, which means you may be making the wrong impression without realizing it. More and more, people are using search engines like Google to get a sense of potential employers, colleagues, or employees, and the impression you make online can have a strong impact on how you are perceived. According to CareerBuilder.com, 60 percent of employers search for information on candidates on social media sites.[6]

Glassdoor.com offers the following tips for how to avoid your social media activity from sabotaging your career success:

1. Check your privacy settings. Ensure that your photos and posts are accessible only to the friends or contacts you want to see them. You want to come across as professional and reliable.
2. Rather than avoiding social media while searching for a job, use it to your advantage. Give future employees a sense of your professional interest by "liking" pages or joining groups of professional organizations related to your career goals.
3. Grammar counts. Be attentive to the quality of writing in all your posts and comments.
4. Be consistent. With each social media outlet, there is a different focus and tone of what you are communicating. LinkedIn is very professional, while Facebook is far more social and relaxed. It's okay to take a different tone on various social media sites, but be sure you aren't blatantly contradicting yourself.
5. Choose your username carefully. Remember, social media may be the first impression someone has of you in the professional realm.[7]

STRIKE A POSE: WORKING AS A FOOD PHOTOGRAPHER

Glenn Jenkins.
Courtesy of Glenn Jenkins

Glenn Jenkins has been a freelance prop stylist for more than twenty years with a wide variety of clients. He works in California's Bay Area as well as in other cities around the country. His clients include a variety of restaurants and magazines, catalogs, and book publishers, most of them with a focus on food and interiors.

What is a typical day in your job?

There are a few parts to my job. There is a lot of preparation that goes into each day of photography. It might mean pulling props from my collection or shopping and sourcing rentals to create the look the client is asking for. Sometimes we create custom surfaces and backgrounds for them and source specific dinnerware or florals.

Usually communicating with the art director, photographer, and client to see what they have in mind and reading the recipes and checking in with the food stylist to see what the ideas are for plating recipes and what they might need from me.

The other part of my job is on set: Organizing the props and setting up the sets based on the order of the shot list. Going over the recipes to confirm we have what we need in the size or material, color, etc. Making sure the things move smoothly between shots.

What's the best part of your job?

I really enjoy the collaboration on most jobs. Getting to work with other creatives, bouncing ideas off each other and being inspired by their vision. I'll often bring props thinking they are for a certain shot or purpose and someone else on the team will see a completely different way to pull things together from what I have brought. I also love to shop. I have a thing for collecting ceramics that I sometimes wonder borders on obsession. Luckily this job provides good cover for that.

What's the worst part of your job?

The job has many decidedly unglamorous moments. I'm often up hours before the rest of the team, shopping at the flower market, making stops at storage units, loading and unloading my car. I have an amazing team helping me, but we often get dragged down into the logistics of the work that can be rather challenging.

Traversing city traffic, difficulties with studios without elevators or space to work, huge locations that have us running between sets. . . . There is often a tension between providing the props needed to fulfill the vision of the client and the budget available to do it. Sometimes they are in conflict and we just have to do our best.

What's the most surprising thing about your job?

The level of specialty in this field has been a surprise. I didn't realize I would be able to make a living focused on food-related photography. I just happened to be in a city with a tremendous amount of opportunity and creativity revolving around the gorgeous foods grown here and the culinary world that has been created. And the diversity within this specialty is also amazing. One week creating custom bread-boards for burgers for a national chain restaurant and then sourcing blooms and nuts for ingredients candle scents, and the next day shopping at gorgeous home stores for the perfect plate for a recipe for an edible cannabis cookbook.

What's next? Where do you see yourself going from here?

I don't really have my next step planned out. I am still very much enjoying the world I am in, but I do see change in the industry coming from a few different directions and I want to be prepared. So I'd better get on that.

Did your education prepare you for the job?

I have an art history degree and I think it truly did prepare me. A solid background in fine art taught me so much about composition and light and space. Working in different mediums prepared me for creating and painting faux finishes that come in handy for backgrounds and surfaces. Color, texture, and knowledge of different periods in art history inform decisions that get made every day.

Is the job what you expected?

I came to this job after many years in retail environments. I worked in NYC doing windows for Bloomingdale's and in San Francisco doing in-store displays for Macy's. I had a good sense of what the job would be like, but I had no idea I would end up where I am today.

Dressing Appropriately

How you dress for a job interview is very important to the impression you want to make. Remember that no matter what the actual environment in which you'd be working, the interview is your chance to present your most professional self. Although you will not likely ever wear a suit to work in a kitchen, for an interview it's the most professional choice. Business casual is also an option—a sport coat for men or blouse for a woman is appropriate, according to Shoes for Crews Europe, which offers advice specifically for what to wear at a chef interview.[8]

If you are applying for a job as a chef, you may be asked to do a demonstration of your cooking, in which case you'd want to dress more comfortably. In that case, it's a good idea to pack a bag of clothing to change into for that segment of the interview.

Hygiene is very important at any interview, but when you are seeking a job preparing and serving food it's paramount that you focus on being clean and well-groomed. If you have long hair, it's a good idea to tie it back. If you wear makeup, keep it light and subtle.

What Employers Expect

Hiring managers and human resource professionals will also have certain expectations of you at an interview. The main thing is preparation: it cannot be overstated that you should arrive to an interview appropriately dressed, on time, unhurried, and ready to answer—and ask—questions.

In any job interview, you should:

- Have a thorough understanding of the organization and the job for which you are applying.
- Be prepared to answer questions about yourself and your relevant experience.
- Be poised and likeable, but still professional. Employers will be looking for a sense of what it would be like to work with you on a daily basis and how your presence would fit in the culture of the business.
- Stay engaged. Listen carefully to what is being asked and offer thoughtful but concise answers. Don't blurt out answers you've memorized; instead, really focus on what is being asked.

- Be prepared to ask your own questions. It shows how much you understand the flow of an organization or workplace and how you will contribute to it. Some questions you can ask include:
  - o What created the need to fill this position? Is it a new position or has someone left the company?
  - o Where does this position fit in the overall hierarchy of the organization?
  - o What are the key skills required to succeed in this job?
  - o What challenges might I expect to face within the first six months on the job?
  - o How does this position relate to the achievement of the company's (or department's, or boss's) goals?
  - o How would you describe the company culture?

IF YOU BELIEVE YOU CAN DO IT, YOU CAN!

Ellen Muckstadt.
Courtesy of Ellen Muckstadt

Ellen Muckstadt began her career in retail when she managed a women's clothing store. From there she had jobs of convenience while raising her family. Eventually she became a private investigator and then a newspaper photographer. She opened her own photography business before taking time off to win a war against breast cancer. After that, she came up with her restaurant plan *in* Milford, New Hampshire. She is very active in her community and spends a lot of time at the gym and outdoors, travels extensively, and thoroughly enjoys any time she can get with her grandchildren. She thinks education is very important—and that there is always something new to learn and that if you believe you can do it, you can.

What is a typical day in your job?

I am in the process of opening my first restaurant. This is a new venture for me. I don't have experience in the culinary field except for cooking three meals a day for my family for the past thirty-five years. Even when we have traveled as a family, rented vacation homes everywhere, I cooked. I have always loved to cook for people. So here I am, opening a restaurant. Presently, a typical day is all about remodeling a store. I have spent the last three weeks, fifteen hours a day, painting, cleaning, ordering, planning, and putting together my place. Although I am exhausted, haven't worn makeup in days, am running out of painting clothes, and ache from head to toe, I love every minute of it!

What's the best part of your job

The best part of my job is watching my business plan take shape. My concept has evolved from the initial plan to make chowder for fairs and farmer's markets to creating a space where I can do that and more. I love the community feel and the enthusiasm from all of my friends, family, and even strangers. I meet someone new every day and share my excitement.

What's the worst part of your job?

The worst part of my job is the uncertainty. Although I am learning as I go, the financial commitment for my startup is a bit scary and will continue to be until I am actually up and running and making money.

What's the most surprising thing about your job?

The most surprising thing about my job is all that I have learned in such a short amount of time. I took a food safety course with ServSafe and don't know how I've been cooking all of these years without that information. I think everyone should take the course and will require it of anyone who wants to work in my restaurant.

What's next? Where do you see yourself going from here?

Shark Tank. I see myself being on *Shark Tank.* I have a concept that could potentially grow, and I will need assistance to take it to a higher level.

Did your education prepare you for the job?

No. My oldest son has said, "Mom, you have had more jobs that you are not qualified for!" I think curiosity, passion, perseverance, and confidence, along with a willingness to learn new things, has given me what I need for this job. I also have a nephew who went to culinary school. I often reach out to him with questions and for advice. He has been a huge help.

Is the job what you expected?

So far, it is. I cannot wait to actually start cooking and take this business model to its potential.

Summary

Congratulations on working through the book! You should now have a strong idea of your career goals within the culinary arts and how to realize them. This chapter discussed how to present yourself as the right candidate to a potential employer—and these strategies are also relevant if you are applying to a college or cooking school or for another form of training.

Here are some tips to sum it up:

- Your résumé should be concise and focused on only relevant aspects of your work experience or education. Although you can include some personal hobbies or details, they should be related to the job and your qualifications for it. For example, if you are applying for a job in an Italian restaurant and you speak fluent Italian, that's certainly something to include.
- Take your time with all your professional documents—your résumé, your cover letter, your LinkedIn profile—and be sure to proofread very carefully to avoid embarrassing and sloppy mistakes.
- Prepare yourself for an interview by anticipating the types of questions you will be asked and coming up with professional and meaningful responses.
- Prepare some questions to ask your potential employer at the interview. This will show that you have a good understanding of and interest in the organization and what role you would have in it.
- Always follow up after an interview with a letter or an e-mail. And e-mail is the fastest way to express your gratitude for the interviewer's time and restate your interest in the position.
- Dress appropriately for an interview and pay extra attention to tidiness and hygiene.
- Be wary of what you share on social media sites while job searching. Most employers research candidates online, and what you have shared will influence their idea of who you are and what it would be like to work with you.

The culinary arts field is broad and exciting, with many different types of jobs and work environments. This book has described the various jobs and provided examples of real working professionals and their impressions of what they do and how they prepared—through education or training—to do it.

Hopefully this will further inspire you to identify your goal and know how to achieve it.

You've chosen a field that is expected to grow in the coming years and one that will offer a creative, diverse, competitive, exciting career path. People will always enjoy preparing, eating, and sharing food, and with a career in the culinary arts you can take part in providing those experiences. Good luck to you for great success in your future.

Glossary

apprentice: A person who is working to gain experience and who generally does anything from prep work to washing dishes.

apprenticeship: A type of job training in which the person being trained is guided by a master of a particular trade, such as cooking.

bachelor's degree: A four-year degree awarded by a college or university.

baker: A person who bakes and sells bread, pastries, and cakes. Bakers work in bakeries or supermarkets and as freelancers, among other places.

beverage manager: A person responsible for the beverage services in restaurants and other food and beverage establishments.

business model: A map for the successful creation and operation of a business, including sources of revenue, target customer base, products, and details of financing.

campus: The location of a school, college, or university.

career assessment test: A test that asks questions particularly geared to identify skills and interests to help inform the test taker about what type of career would suit him or her.

caterer: A person who designs the menu and prepares food for parties, for example, weddings, birthdays, or corporate events.

chef: A trained cook who prepares food and often manages a kitchen. Chefs work in restaurants, diners, spas, hotels, schools, and private homes—wherever food is served.

chef de cuisine: This is the highest position in the modern kitchen. The chef de cuisine is in charge of everything from menu preparation to ordering ingredients.

chef de partie: A chef de partie—there are several in a professional kitchen—is a chef who is responsible for a particular station. There will be several parties—such as a fish chef, vegetable chef, sauté chef, or pastry chef. Parties often have a cuisinier, commis, or apprentices working with them.

colleagues: The people with whom you work.

commis: A junior cook assigned to a particular station, most often responsible for ensuring the proper cooking equipment is present at his or her station.

community college: A two-year college that confers associate's degrees.

cover letter: A document that usually accompanies a résumé and allows candidates applying to a job or a school or an internship the opportunity to describe their motivation and qualifications.

cuisinier: The cuisiniers do the actual cooking at a specific station.

culinary arts school: An institution devoted to education in the art and science of cooking and food preparation.

customer service: The process of taking care of a customer's needs.

delicatessen or deli: A small shop that sells high-quality foods, such as types of cheese and cold cooked meat.

entrepreneur: A person who creates, launches, and manages his or her own business.

financial aid: Various means of receiving financial support for the purposes of attending school. This can be a grant or scholarship, for example.

food photographer: A trained photographer whose job it is to set up photo shoots and capture images of food.

foodie: A person who is passionate about food and enjoys a variety of cooking styles and cuisine.

food service manager: A person who is responsible for the daily operation of restaurants and other establishments that prepare and serve food.

food truck: A vehicle equipped to cook and sell food. Food trucks are often equipped with kitchens for preparing food, such as hamburgers or hot dogs.

freelancer: A person who owns his or her own business providing services for a variety of clients.

gap year: A year between high school and higher education or employment during which a person can explore his or her passions and interests, often while traveling.

Industrial Revolution: The changes in manufacturing and transportation that began with fewer things being made by hand. The Industrial Revolution had a big impact on how food was prepared and served.

internship: A work experience opportunity that lasts for a set period of time and can be paid or unpaid.

interpersonal skills: The ability to communicate and interact with other people in an effective manner.

interview: A part of the job-seeking process in which a candidate meets with a potential employer, usually face to face, in order to discuss his or her work experience and education and seek information about the position.

kitchen brigade: An organization of the hierarchy of all members of a staff working in a professional kitchen.

line cook: A line cook is employed in restaurants and other kitchens and prepares a lot of the food, working under a head chef.

locally grown: Foods that are grown, processed, and sold within a certain region or area.

major: The subject or course of study in which you choose to earn your degree.

master's degree: A degree that is sought by those who have already earned a bachelor's degree in order to further their education.

Michelin star: A rating system identifying the best upscale restaurants around the world.

networking: The processes of building, strengthening, and maintaining professional relationships as a way to further your career goals.

on-the-job training: A type of training in which a person is learning while actually doing the job in a real-world environment.

organic: Food that is produced via a farming system that does not use pesticides or man-made fertilizers or livestock feed additives.

pop-up restaurant: A restaurant based in a temporary location.

restaurateur: A person who owns and manages the operation of a restaurant.

résumé: A document, usually one page, that outlines a person's professional experience and education, designed to give potential employers a sense of a candidate's qualifications.

social media: Websites and applications that enable users to create and share content online for networking and social-sharing purposes. Examples include Facebook and Instagram.

sous chef de cuisine: In the French language, *sous* means *under*—making the sous chef a sort of deputy to the chef de cuisine. The sous chef is second in command in the kitchen, taking over the responsibilities of the head chef in his or her absence.

vocational school: A school at which students learn how to do a job that requires special skills, such as cooking.

work culture: A concept that defines the beliefs, philosophy, thought processes, and attitudes of employees in a particular organization.

Notes

Introduction: So You Want a Career in the Culinary Arts

1. Bureau of Labor Statistics, US Department of Labor, "Chefs and Head Cooks," *Occupational Outlook Handbook*, www.bls.gov/ooh/food-preparation-and-serving/chefs-and-head-cooks.htm.

2. Bureau of Labor Statistics, US Department of Labor, "Food Preparation Workers," *Occupational Outlook Handbook*, www.bls.gov/ooh/food-preparation-and-serving/food-preparation-workers.htm.

3. Best Choice Schools, "What Is the Employment Outlook for the Field of Culinary Arts?" www.bestchoiceschools.com/faq/what-is-the-employment-outlook-for-the-field-of-culinary-arts.

Chapter 1

1. Online Etymology Dictionary, "Restaurant," www.etymonline.com/word/restaurant.

2. Sarah R. Labensky, Priscilla Martel, and Alan M. Hause, *On Cooking: A Textbook of Culinary Fundamentals*, 5th ed. (New York: Pearson, 2011). https://www.slideshare.net/rohitmohan754/ch-01-a-culinary-history.

3. EricT_CulinaryLore, "What Is the Kitchen Brigade?" *Culinary Lore*, March 4, 2014, https://culinarylore.com/food-history:what-is-the-kitchen-brigade.

4. *Michelin Guide*, "History of the *Michelin Guide*," https://guide.michelin.com/sg/history-of-the-michelin-guide-sg.

5. Bureau of Labor Statistics, https://data.bls.gov/search/query/results?cx=013738036195919377644%3A6ih0hfrgl50&q=food+service+inurl%3Abls.gov%2Fooh%2F.

6. PayScale, "Average Executive Chef Salary," www.payscale.com/research/US /Job=Executive_Chef/Salary.

7. Careerlancer, "How to Become a Freelance Baker," https://careerlancer.net /become-freelance-baker.

Chapter 2

1. DO-IT, "Preparing for a Career: An Online Tutorial," www.washington.edu /doit/preparing-career-online-tutorial.

2. Bureau of Labor Statistics, US Department of Labor, "Chefs and Head Cooks," *Occupational Outlook Handbook*, www.bls.gov/ooh/food-preparation-and -serving/chefs-and-head-cooks.htm.

3. Bureau of Labor Statistics, US Department of Labor, "Cooks," *Occupational Outlook Handbook*, www.bls.gov/ooh/food-preparation-and-serving/cooks.htm.

4. Bureau of Labor Statistics, US Department of Labor, "Career and Technical Education Teachers," *Occupational Outlook Handbook*, www.bls.gov/ooh/education -training-and-library/career-and-technical-education-teachers.htm.

5. Bureau of Labor Statistics, US Department of Education, "How to Become a Chef or Head Cook," *Occupational Outlook Handbook*, www.bls.gov/ooh/food -preparation-and-serving/chefs-and-head-cooks.htm#tab-4.

6. CulinarySchools.org, "Culinary Degrees School Finder," www.culinaryschools .org/culinary-degree-types.

7. Bureau of Labor Statistics, US Department of Labor, "Agricultural and Food Scientists," *Occupational Outlook Handbook*, www.bls.gov/ooh/life-physical-and-social -science/agricultural-and-food-scientists.htm.

8. Bureau of Labor Statistics, US Department of Labor, "Food Service Managers," *Occupational Outlook Handbook*, www.bls.gov/ooh/management/food-service -managers.htm.

9. Bureau of Labor Statistics, US Department of Labor, "Dietitians and Nutritionists," *Occupational Outlook Handbook*, http://www.bls.gov/ooh/healthcare /dietitians-and-nutritionists.htm.

10. Culinary Institute of America, "Study Abroad Experiences," www.ciachef.edu /travel-experiences.

11. Madeline Stone, "At 16, Chef Flynn McGarry Is Living on His Own in New York and Running a One-Man Pop-up Restaurant That's Booked Solid," *Business Insider*, September 17, 2015, www.businessinsider.com/16-year-old-chef-flynn-mcgarry-takes -nyc-by-storm-2015-9.

Chapter 3

1. Steven R. Antonoff, "College Personality Quiz," *U.S. News & World Report,* July 31, 2018, www.usnews.com/education/best-colleges/right-school/choices/articles/college-personality-quiz.

2. Stephen G. Jones, "Culinary School Mistake: Not Looking at Accreditation," The Reluctant Gourmet, January 16, 2016, www.reluctantgourmet.com/culinary-school-mistake-accreditation.

3. Culinary Corps, http://culinarycorps.org/; Cooking Matters, AmeriCorps, https://cookingmatters.org/americorps.

4. EducationCostHelper.com, "Culinary School Costs," https://education.costhelper.com/culinary-schools.html.

5. FAFSA, "Apply for Aid," https://studentaid.ed.gov/sa/fafsa.

Chapter 4

1. Bradford Hall Career Institute, "A Culinary Arts Sample Résumé," www.branfordhall.edu/a-culinary-arts-sample-resume.

2. Melissa King, "How to Write a Good Culinary Arts Résumé," The Nest, https://woman.thenest.com/write-good-culinary-arts-resume-11024.html.

3. Alison Doyle, "Student Resume Examples and Templates," The Balance Careers, October 5, 2018, www.thebalancecareers.com/student-resume-examples-and-templates-2063555.

4. Joshua Waldman, *Job Searching with Social Media for Dummies* (Hoboken, NJ: John Wiley and Sons, 2013).

5. Alison Doyle, "A List of Interview Questions for Chefs," The Balance Careers, May 25, 2018, www.thebalancecareers.com/chef-interview-questions-2061467.

6. Career Builder, "Number of Employers Using Social Media to Screen Candidates Has Increased 500 Percent over the Last Decade," press release, April 28, 2016, www.careerbuilder.com/share/aboutus/pressreleasesdetail.aspx?ed=12%2F31%2F2016&id=pr945&sd=4%2F28%2F2016.

7. Alice E. M. Underwood, "9 Things to Avoid on Social Media While Looking for a New Job," Glassdoor, June 3, 2018, www.glassdoor.com/blog/things-to-avoid-on-social-media-job-search.

8. Shoes for Crews Europe, "What Should Chefs Wear to an Interview?" Shoes for Crews, July 12, 2017, https://blog.sfceurope.com/what-should-chefs-wear-to-an-interview

Further Resources

*T*he following websites, magazines, and organizations can help you further investigate and educate yourself on topics related to a culinary arts career, all of which will help you as you take the next steps in your career, now and throughout.

Professional Organizations

American Culinary Federation (ACF)
www.acfchefs.org
ACF is an organization for professional chefs and cooks. It is the largest such organization in North America, and currently has approximately fifteen thousand members. Its mission, according to its website, is to be the "standard of excellence for the culinary industry, advancing and promoting professionalism, leadership and collaboration." Visit its website to learn of high school and post–high school accredited culinary arts programs.

Cooking Matters
http://cookingmatters.org
Cooking Matters is an initiative of AmeriCorps, through which AmeriCorps members assist partners across the United States to help families on tight budgets prepare and enjoy healthy, affordable meals. This includes anything from guided tours of supermarkets to cooking classes and other educational tools. Anyone—including kids and teens—can participate in helping American families eat and live better.

CulinaryCorps
http://culinarycorps.org
As its motto, "Good Food Doing Good" indicates, CulinaryCorps recruits volunteer chefs to participate in programs in various communities in the United

States. Since its inception in 2006, CulinaryCorps has recruited more than 150 chef volunteers for eleven weeklong volunteer trips to New Orleans, Mississippi, Maine, and Puerto Rico.

Culinary Institute of America (CIA)
www.ciachef.edu
Since its founding in 1946, the CIA has become a leader of excellence in culinary arts education. With campuses in New York, California, Texas, and Singapore, the CIA strives to provide the highest level of quality with its programs, and to raise awareness of all issues facing the food industry, from health to sustainability.

Food Tank
https://foodtank.com
The self-proclaimed "think tank for food," Food Tank provides information regarding sustainability and food change. Members help support a global community for healthy, safe eaters, and to educate, inspire, advocate, and create change in the food system.

Future Chefs
https://futurechefs.net
The mission of Future Chefs is to prepare young people interested in the culinary arts as a career to achieve their goal after completing high school. Launched as a school-to-career program in 2008, the Boston-based initiative prepares youth for a career in a range of culinary arts careers.

International Association of Culinary Professionals (IACP)
www.iacp.com
The IACP is a professional organization with a membership that includes food writers, photographers, stylists, bloggers, marketers, nutritionists, chefs, restaurateurs, culinary tour operators, artisan food producers, and academics. Members have access to events, blogs, conferences, a membership directory, and other resources to help them advance their careers.

James Beard Foundation
www.jamesbeard.org
James Beard was a cookbook author and cooking instructor who championed American cuisine. The foundation in his name is a New York–based nonprofit. Members have access to food news, recipes, and other culinary-related information via the foundation's blog. You can also subscribe to the foundation's digital newsletter, *Beard Bites*.

Peace Corps
www.peacecorps.gov
If you are interested in taking a gap year before taking the next step in your career or education, consider joining the Peace Corps. Volunteers have the experience of working on projects that relate to health, agriculture, education, and youth and development, just to name a few, and the experience can help you find your passion and understand what the next step in your life should be.

Research Chefs Association (RCA)
www.culinology.org
An association for research chefs, RCA was founded in 1996 and now has more than two thousand members. It strives to be the leading source of culinary and technical information to the food industry, with a membership that includes chefs, food scientists, and other culinary arts professionals who inform the future of food research and development.

United States Personal Chef Organization (USPCO)
www.uspca.com
The USPCO provides continuing education to members, as well as advice to individuals interested in becoming personal chefs. Members also enjoy insurance discounts, access to a blog, conferences, and other resources.

Women Chefs and Restaurateurs (WCR)
https://womenchefs.org
Barbara Tropp and seven other pioneering women chefs and restaurateurs founded the WCR to be an "active resource for women seeking to advance

culinary education and gain recognition in various areas of the food and beverage industry." The result is a strong network of professional women in the culinary arts field.

Your Culinary World
www.yourculinaryworld.com
Husband and wife Peter Schlagel and Ana Kinkaid share news about contemporary wine and cuisine on their site, including notable events; culinary education news; cookbook, restaurant, and destination advice; and more. You can sign up on their site to subscribe to their newsletter.

Magazines

Chef Magazine
www.chefmagazine.com
Chef magazine is aimed at food service professionals and provides content to inform decisions for their businesses. With articles about everything from food to food service equipment, it provides information on a wide variety of topics, including business solutions, ingredient usages, management tips, and up-to-date news on beverage trends.

Epicurious
www.epicurious.com
The go-to online resource for anyone who likes to cook, from the earliest beginner to the seasoned pro, *Epicurious* provides food-related articles, recipes, menu plans, advice on kitchen appliances, and more. Definitely a good resource for the future chef.

Food Service News
www.foodservicenews.net
A source of news for restaurants and the food service industry as a whole, *Food Service News* provides content to subscribers about restaurants, chefs, conferences, equipment, and feature stories that inform on news and trends related to the industry.

Nation's Restaurant News
www.nrn.com
Nation's Restaurant News is the source for business news and intelligence in the food service industry. It claims to have the largest editorial team in the industry, which delivers timely, up-to-date content to serve the largest overall audience in the industry.

Vegetarian Times
www.vegetariantimes.com
An online magazine aimed at foodies who prefer a vegetarian or vegan diet (and those who cook for them), *Vegetarian Times* provides information on recipes, health, life and garden news, ingredients, kitchen tools, and more.

Bibliography

Antonoff, Steven R. "College Personality Quiz." *U.S. News & World Report*, July 31, 2018. Retrieved October 15, 2018, from www.usnews.com/education/best-colleges/right-school/choices/articles/college-personality-quiz.

Best Choice Schools. "What Is the Employment Outlook for the Field of Culinary Arts?" Retrieved October 15, 2018, from www.bestchoice schools.com/faq/what-is-the-employment-outlook-for-the-field-of-culinary-arts.

Bradford Hall Career Institute. "A Culinary Arts Sample Résumé." Retrieved October 15, 2018, from www.branfordhall.edu/a-culinary-arts-sample-resume.

Bureau of Labor Statistics, US Department of Labor. "Agricultural and Food Scientists." *Occupational Outlook Handbook*. Retrieved October 15, 2018, from www.bls.gov/ooh/life-physical-and-social-science/agricultural-and-food-scientists.htm.

———. "Career and Technical Education Teachers." *Occupational Outlook Handbook*. Retrieved October 15, 2018, from www.bls.gov/ooh/education-training-and-library/career-and-technical-education-teachers.htm.

———. "Chefs and Head Cooks." *Occupational Outlook Handbook*. Retrieved October 15, 2018, from www.bls.gov/ooh/food-preparation-and-serving/chefs-and-head-cooks.htm.

———. "Cooks." *Occupational Outlook Handbook*. Retrieved October 15, 2018, from www.bls.gov/ooh/food-preparation-and-serving/cooks.htm.

———. "Dietitians and Nutritionists." *Occupational Outlook Handbook*. Retrieved October 15, 2018, from http://www.bls.gov/ooh/healthcare/dietitians-and-nutritionists.htm.

———. "Food Preparation Workers." *Occupational Outlook Handbook*. Retrieved October 15, 2018, from www.bls.gov/ooh/food-preparation-and-serving/food-preparation-workers.htm.

———. "Food Service Managers." *Occupational Outlook Handbook*. Retrieved October 15, 2018, from www.bls.gov/ooh/management/food-service-managers.htm.

————. "How to Become a Chef or Head Cook." *Occupational Outlook Handbook*. Retrieved October 15, 2018, from www.bls.gov/ooh/food -preparation-and-serving/chefs-and-head-cooks.htm#tab-4.

Career Builder. "Number of Employers Using Social Media to Screen Candidates Has Increased 500 Percent over the Last Decade." Press release, April 28, 2016. Retrieved October 15, 2018, from www.career builder.com/share/aboutus/pressreleasesdetail.aspx?ed=12%2F31%2F20 16&id=pr945&sd=4%2F28%2F2016.

Careerlancer. "How to Become a Freelance Baker." Retrieved October 15, 2018, from https://careerlancer.net/become-freelance-baker.

College Board. "Types of College Loans." Retrieved October 15, 2018, from https://bigfuture.collegeboard.org/pay-for-college/loans/types-of-college -loans.

Cooking Matters. "AmeriCorps." Retrieved October 15, 2018, from https:// cookingmatters.org/americorps.

CulinarySchols.org. "Culinary Degrees School Finder." Retrieved October 15, 2018, from www.culinaryschools.org/culinary-degree-types.

Culinary Institute of America. "Study Abroad Experiences." Retrieved October 15, 2018, from www.ciachef.edu/travel-experiences.

DO-IT. "Preparing for a Career: An Online Tutorial." Retrieved October 15, 2018, from www.washington.edu/doit/preparing-career-online-tutorial.

Doyle, Alison. "A List of Interview Questions for Chefs." The Balance Careers, May 25, 2018. Retrieved October 15, 2018, from www.thebalancecareers .com/chef-interview-questions-2061467.

————. "Student Résumé Examples and Templates." The Balance Careers, October 5, 2018. Retrieved October 15, 2018, from www.thebalance careers.com/student-resume-examples-and-templates-2063555.

EducationCostHelper.com. "Culinary School Costs." Retrieved October 15, 2018, from https://education.costhelper.com/culinary-schools.html.

Educations.com. "Online Career Test." Retrieved October 15, 2018, from www.educations.com/career-test.

EricT_CulinaryLore. "What Is the Kitchen Brigade?" Culinary Lore, March 4, 2014. Retrieved October 15, 2018, from https://culinarylore.com/ food-history:what-is-the-kitchen-brigade.

E-rcps.com. "A Career in Culinary Arts?" Retrieved October 15, 2018, from www.e-rcps.com/learn.

Federal Student Aid. "Grants and Scholarships Are Free Money to Help Pay for College or Career School." Retrieved October 15, 2018, from https://studentaid.ed.gov/types/grants-scholarships.

GoCollege.com. "Types of Scholarships." Retrieved October 15, 2018, from www.gocollege.com/financial-aid/scholarships/types.

Jones, Stephen G. "Culinary School Mistake: Not Looking at Accreditation." The Reluctant Gourmet, January 16, 2016. Retrieved October 15, 2018, from www.reluctantgourmet.com/culinary-school-mistake-accreditation.

King, Melissa. "How to Write a Good Culinary Arts Resume." The Nest. Retrieved October 15, 2018, from https://woman.thenest.com/write-good-culinary-arts-resume-11024.html.

Labensky, Sarah R., Priscilla Martel, and Alan M. Hause. On Cooking: A Textbook of Culinary Fundamentals. 5th Ed. New York: Pearson. 2011.

Michelin Guide. "History of the Michelin Guide." Retrieved October 15, 2018, from https://guide.michelin.com/sg/history-of-the-michelin-guide-sg.

Online Etymology Dictionary. "Restaurant." Retrieved October 15, 2018, www.etymonline.com/word/restaurant.

PayScale. "Average Executive Chef Salary." Retrieved October 15, 2018, from www.payscale.com/research/US/Job=Executive_Chef/Salary.

Princeton Review. "Career Quiz." Retrieved October 15, 2018, from www.princetonreview.com/quiz/career-quiz.

Shoes for Crews Europe. "What Should Chefs Wear to an Interview?" Shoes for Crews, July 12, 2017. Retrieved October 15, 2018, from https://blog.sfceurope.com/what-should-chefs-wear-to-an-interview.

Stone, Madeline. "At 16, Chef Flynn McGarry Is Living on His Own in New York and Running a One-Man Pop-up Restaurant That's Booked Solid." Business Insider, September 17, 2015. Retrieved October 15, 2018 from, www.businessinsider.com/16-year-old-chef-flynn-mcgarry-takes-nyc-by-storm-2015-9.

Underwood, Alice E. M. "9 Things to Avoid on Social Media While Looking for a New Job." Glassdoor, June 3, 2018. Retrieved October 15, 2018, from www.glassdoor.com/blog/things-to-avoid-on-social-media-job-search.

Waldman, Joshua. Job Searching with Social Media for Dummies. Hoboken, NJ: Wiley, 2013.

About the Author

Tracy Brown Hamilton is a writer, editor, and journalist based in the Netherlands. She has written several books on topics ranging from careers to media and economics to pop culture. She lives with her husband and three children.

EDITORIAL BOARD